PENGUINS

PENGUINS

John Sparks and Tony Soper

Illustrated by Robert Gillmor

Facts On File Publications
New York, New York ● Oxford, England

√**RAP.** *227 0322*

Library of Cataloging in Publication Data

Sparks, John
  Penguins

  Bibliography: p.
  Includes index.
  1. Penguins.   I. Soper, Tony.   II. Title.
QL696.S473S63   1987   598.4′41   86-29063
ISBN 0-8160-1753-0

First published in the United States of America by
Facts On File, Inc. 460 Park Avenue South, New York,
New York 10016.

Printed in Great Britain

10   9   8   7   6   5   4   3   2   1

Contents

Introduction

Who would believe in penguins,
unless he had seen them?
CONOR O BRIEN
Across Three Oceans

And having seen them, how would he know what they were? The first men to see penguins were hard put to it to classify them, although as their interest was mainly gastronomic it did not matter too much. But they were curious. The animal was flightless, yet it had a head and beak of a bird. It moved like a clumsy man on the land but in the sea it became a joyous cavorting fish. No wonder the early explorers were confused, and they variously wrote it off as fowl, beast or fish as it suited them. Certainly it was convenient to regard them as fish, so the penguin joined the beaver and the barnacle goose as a dish technically suitable for dinner on Friday.

Penguins are flightless because their way of life makes flight superfluous. They had few enemies on land till man came on the scene, and they directed their talents to becoming supremely adapted to the aquatic hunting life. Of all birds they are the most expert in the water. And although it is *strictly* true to say that they are flightless, truth is mocked when the bird leaps into the water. For the penguin flies underwater with the total mastery of a beast in its element. Its narrow scaly flippers, with flattened bones, become paddles, and its feet act as planes and rudders. Whereas the aerial bird gains lift from the downward component of its wing action,

7

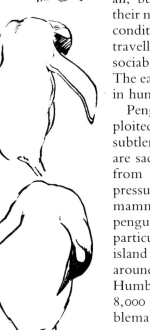

the penguin shoots forward on the upward stroke. And it flies through the water at a good speed, 18km per hour (10 knots) or more. When it needs to breathe it 'flies' up to the surface and leaps clear, flippers flailing, and plunges again to chase cuttlefish and crustaceans. The distribution of the penguin, in fact, is closely related to the fertile currents spreading northwards from the southern Polar continent. Of the seventeen species, only two are truly Antarctic, five belong to the icy sub-Antarctic regions, six to southern temperate regions and four to the sub-tropics. The tropical species survive only as far north as the cool Antarctic-born currents. An invisible barrier of equatorial warmth denies them access to the northern hemisphere.

In the sea, the penguin is a master mariner, out of it he becomes our lovable-ludicrous Little Man in formal dress. Upright, he waddles, hops or runs to his spartan nest in a cave, burrow or out in the open. Two species build no nest at all, but cradle the solitary egg against their tarsi, walking their nest territory with them and incubating in harsh climatic conditions which would daunt the most intrepid human travellers. Most penguins are gregarious, living in raucous sociability in rookeries of as many as a million individuals. The early seafarers killed them like flies and later boiled them in hundreds of thousands for their oil.

Penguin populations are so large that, unlike some exploited species, they have survived to face the new and ever subtler dangers of the present day. Some species, however, are sadly declining. Yellow-eyed penguins are withdrawing from the New Zealand mainland in the face of human pressure, and the depredations of a bevy of carnivorous mammals introduced by us. The South African jackass penguin has taken a hammering from oil spillages, a particularly unpleasant form of pollution visited upon the island rookeries by the steady stream of supertankers forging around the Cape of Good Hope. Even the South American Humboldt penguin has been reduced to between 6,000 and 8,000 pairs, rendering its long-term survival a little problematical. Although the Antarctic kinds are faring well at the moment, toxic chemical residues have reached even those remote parts of the globe and have contaminated the indigenous wildlife.

But even 'on the ice' a raucous, musty-smelling penguin rookery is given high priority on the intinerary of all VIPs. The visitor gawps at the birds and then scatters them, nest and eggs and all, with the fierce down-draught of his helicopter blades. But who wouldn't grasp at the chance of a few hours in a penguin rookery? Penguins are one of the few remaining creatures which are not afraid of us, and show interest instead of fear. How rewarding to be free of the accursed invisible barrier which separates us from other animals and causes them to keep their distance so pointedly. Penguins, in their loud-voiced thousands, always seem in party mood to the human observer. The scientists even allow themselves to consider the possibility that adélie penguins are playing games on the ice and have a special version of ice-floe 'touch'. They jostle one another for the chance to take a free ride on a conveniently passing ice floe, only to jump off and join the queue again for another ride, a performance which seems to have no other object but fun.

It is difficult to be solemn about penguins. Their stance and behaviour are a caricature of man. We cannot help seeing ourselves reflected in them and we cannot help taking an anthropomorphic view of them. If they had been known to us earlier, it is safe to assume they would have played an important role in folklore. Pliny would have written penetrating accounts of their behaviour but classified them firmly as fish, Aesop would surely have devised a chilling encounter between a penguin and a leopard seal. But we are denied all this because European man only discovered the birds round about 1500. And it was many years before the public recognized them and took them to its heart. Early accounts wrote them off as tough, stupid and vicious birds, fit only for the bludgeon and the cauldron. It was not until live penguins reached the European zoos in the nineteenth century that light dawned and people warmed to these much-abused and delightful characters.

Sketches from life of King Penguin preening

9

A large rookery of magellanic penguins at Punta Tombo (*New York Zoological Society*)

Now, of course, they are well up in the 'top ten' of animal favourites at zoos. No general zoo is complete without its band of shuffling penguins. Edinburgh has specialized successfully in penguins for many years, as a result of useful relations with the whaling companies which used Leith as a home port. And at Frankfurt Zoo you can see emperor penguins in a specially designed polar exhibit which involves refrigerated ice and an Antarctic pool. To the best of our knowledge no one actually keeps one as a house-pet, but no doubt someone will sooner or later. Animal dealers occasionally have them for sale, but they cost anything from £850 for a Peruvian to £4,500 for a king penguin and £10,000 for an emperor. And your fish bill would be a shock.

The penguin image has made its trademark heavily in the northern hemisphere, even though the wild creature is absent. Penguins sell biscuits and wool and other sublime irrelevancies. They inhabit the daily cartoon world. Postage stamps carry penguins and public houses are named after them. Even a highly-successful publishing business is built of them: when Sir Allen Lane was looking for a house-mark for his audacious paperback project, it was a secretary who suggested 'Penguin' and, he says, it was immediately and obviously right. The Penguin image was an embodiment of all that the series aimed at – 'dignified flippancy'. King penguins followed, along with Pelicans, Peregrines and Puffins, and we wait for what must surely be Penguin Books ultimate achievement – Emperor Penguins!

Firmly established in our commerical lives, penguins are still favourite subjects for the field scientist. Living in an environment where relatively few other animals become involved in their life-pattern, they are ideal field-laboratory subjects. Zoologists have worked in the Antarctic for many years. And although one writer, many years ago, was rash enough to say that 'the natural history of penguins might now be considered complete', scientific papers come rolling off the presses in ever-increasing numbers. What we have tried to do in this book is to give a broad picture of the known penguin world.

Note to the Revised Edition

Since 1967 when we wrote the first edition of this book, the frontiers of our knowledge about penguins have been considerably advanced. For example, the art of monitoring the activity of individual birds has been refined, with the result that we now know for sure how deep wild penguins dive. The workings of their bodies, the details of their vision, and the impact that their great rookeries have upon the resources of the southern oceans is better understood today than twenty years ago. We have therefore had to revise parts of the text but without sacrificing the aim of the book – to give a broad picture of the penguin's world.

We are, however, no wiser on one matter. There is no unanimity among ornithologists on the question of how many different kinds of penguins share this planet with us! Some say sixteen, others seventeen, and a few maintain that there are eighteen species. It rather depends which zoological roll call you prefer. Some taxonomists prefer to lump the little and white-flippered and the royal and macaroni penguins together so reducing the list to sixteen. Even the most erudite scientists tend to say 'between sixteen and eighteen' . . .

But everyone agrees on one thing: penguins are habit-forming.

JOHN SPARKS
TONY SOPER
1986

1 · Penguins as Birds

An eminent nineteenth-century zoologist once claimed that there was no greater anomaly in nature than a flightless bird. Yet there are several. Penguins, with their leathery quill-less flippers, are the obvious example, but grounded birds exist in many different families; the largest and probably the most spectacular birds ever to have existed were forced to walk this planet by virtue of their grossly inadequate wings. For example *Phororachis*, of South American origin and related to the seriemas and rails, was but one of a number of rapacious carnivores sporting strong, hooked beaks; it strutted the earth about thirty million years ago. The elephant birds of Madagascar were herbivorous and rather like giant ostriches, and some of the moas, known to the seventeenth-century inhabitants of New Zealand, stood 3.5m (12ft) high. Alas, the bones of these fine birds now only adorn museum cases to excite our imagination. Ostriches, rheas, emus, and cassowaries are the largest birds still living and all are flightless, relying upon their size and speed to escape their enemies.

Although for most birds flight is essential as a means of

13

Kiwi

Ostrich

Emu

Rhea

Cassowary

King Penguin

Takahe

Kagu

Flightless Cormorant

Titicaca Grebe

Steamer Duck

avoiding capture by predators, in such places as oceanic islands or larger isolated continents they have found themselves unmolested on the ground, and those species which have not needed to fly in order to secure their food have tended to lose the ability to do so. Take New Zealand, which was not only the stronghold of the moas, but is also the modern centre of penguin diversity. Although Antarctica boasts the greatest concentration of penguin numbers, New Zealand and its associated islands have no less than six species (yellow-eyed, little, erect crested, Fiordland, Snares Island and royal). The bird population of the archipelago includes a couple of flightless rails (the takahe and weka), a grounded, nocturnal parrot (the kakapo) and three species of kiwis, renowned throughout the world as New Zealand's national birds; furthermore, a wattlebird called the kokako rarely makes sustained flights, but vigorously hops from branch to branch, and glides between trees losing much height in the process. Plump, grey steamer ducks, with a range stretching from Chile to the Falkland Islands, the flightless grebe from Lake Titicaca, high in the Andes, and the Galapagos cormorant, are other examples of species which have lived in relative isolation from terrestrial predators and can no longer fly.

Of course, species like the dodo have paid dearly for their flightlessness; they lived on islands which had been protected from carnivorous mammals for millions of years by the sea, but once predatory man, in the form of hungry mariners, had crossed the barrier, within a few years he bludgeoned, salted, and tucked into the entire population. In some cases the predator was man's domestic pets; one cat is said to have had the distinction of exterminating the flightless St Stephens Island wren of New Zealand.

The penguins do, however, constitute the largest family of completely flightless birds. Although here again it could be argued that these are birds which do not need to fly to escape their enemies, this is only part of the story, because their inability to take to the air is connected with their mastery of the sea.

15

Early observers could perhaps be forgiven for thinking that these erect, pompously waddling creatures, so much more at home in the sea than on land, represented a transition stage between fish and birds. In 1620 Admiral Beaulieu, sailing off South Africa, took jackass penguins to be feathered fish with two fins and two paws – though in the same century two other students of penguins did risk the comment that '*Ils sont un mélange de la bête, de l'oiseau et du poisson – mais c'est de l'oiseau qu'ils se rapprochent le plus!*' As late as 1801 they were described as a link between the feathered and the finny tribe. Whether this obsession with the penguins' relationship to fish was merely the result of wishful thinking by protein-hungry Christians is debatable; but certainly some of the amazing stories in the folklore of Christian communities about the origin of different kinds of birds did allow the 'no meat on Fridays' rule to be abused with a righteous conscience! Anyway, surely birds by their very nature could fly? Yet these creatures, as one writer – who unfortunately was only interested in clubbing them to death for the pot – quaintly put it, 'cannot run and fly even worse'. To the early chroniclers, penguins would indeed seem to be clumsy creatures, neither proper birds on the one hand nor fish on the other; but although the subjects have not changed, the zoologist 300 years later paints a very different picture of them.

A penguin is, of course, far from cumbersome when in its true element, the sea. It is in fact an organism which has become perfectly adapted over a long course of evolution for surface diving and swimming. A bird 'designed' to be borne aloft on swirling air currents would be unsuited to swimming in the denser sea, so in becoming suited to the task of sub-aqua flight, the penguin has forfeited the power of aerial progression. (Chapter 5 gives the full story of the evolution of penguins.)

Birds evolved from a group of small reptiles which skipped around on their hind legs some 140 million years ago, during the Triassic period. And although there have been various changes in structure with the effluxion of time, birds remain to a large extent glorified reptiles, because the chief and most important attribute setting them apart from their earthbound ancestors remains the feather. *Archaeopteryx*, the earliest fossil bird to be discovered, would have been relegated to the reptiles on the evidence of its bone structure alone, were it not for the perfect impressions, in the fine lithographic limestone in which it had become entombed, of feathers splaying out from the forelimbs, indicating that they were perfectly good avian wings. Feathers made flight possible because of their large surface area and low weight; but they were probably just as important in enclosing an insulating layer of air next to the body. This insulation allowed these proto-birds to maintain a high body temperature. Like mammals, birds are warm blooded: that is, they have a high and relatively constant temperature, which enables them to live an active life irrespective of the temperatures of the environment. Since birds then do not take up the temperature of their surroundings but carry their own heat around with them, they can penetrate colder areas of the earth, and the adélie and emperor penguins have conspicuously exploited this ability, by living under more rigorous extremes of cold than any other animal.

Most people positively associate penguins with blizzards, and seas dotted with ice floes and so it is generally assumed that all these birds spend their lives in the inhospitable wastes of Antarctica. By and large this is a fallacy, because only two species are truly restricted to Antarctica, although the majority of individuals are probably concentrated within the sub-Antarctic zone. However, the breeding range of penguins does coincide with the cooler parts of the southern oceans, eleven out of the seventeen species belonging to the more temperate regions of the southern hemisphere, with New Zealand and its warmer satellite islands claiming six of them. Each region has its own characteristic temperature range, to which birds confined to the region will be adapted and in which they will live most comfortably. The monthly mean *air* temperature in the *temperate* region varies from several degrees above freezing to nearly 20°C (68°F); these are the temperatures in which the majority of penguin species are

17

adapted to survive. The *sub-Antarctic* zone has no month in which the monthly mean air temperature approaches 8°C (46°F), but at least one-half of the year has a mean monthly temperature above freezing. In the *Antarctic* zone, however, air temperatures never average more than 1·5°C (34·7°F); in the outer maritime areas, where it is moderated by the sea, the winter temperature rarely falls below −10°C (14°F). In the continental Antarctic areas the temperature never exceeds freezing point and in winter it falls well below −20°C (−4°F); these are the areas in which the adélie and emperor breed, though only the emperor faces the Antarctic winter.

Within the southern half of the globe, the penguin family ranges from the Equator to the ice shelf of Antarctica, at 77° S latitude. As all penguins appear to be built upon the same lines, what modifications are necessary to allow some species to live comfortably in frigid conditions whereas others thrive in almost tropical climates?

The body temperature of an adélie penguin sitting out a driving blizzard in Antarctica is similar to that of a Galapagos penguin roasting on a lava flow beneath the fierce equatorial

Galapagos penguins on an island in Elizabeth Bay (*Phillipa Scott*)

sun. Each one is carrying around a similar quantity of heat, and yet the heat-balance problems of adélie and jackass are entirely different; the former must maintain its temperature in a freezing environment, whereas the jackass penguin's problem is to get rid of as much heat as possible in order to prevent its temperature rising to lethal limits. Both have to achieve a correct balance between heat generation within the body, and of heat loss to their surroundings.

Chemical processes involved in digestion and respiration, for example, or the performance of mechanical work by muscles, all liberate considerable quantities of heat and help to keep the body warm. Some of this heat will inevitably leak away into the environment by conduction, convection and radiation. Penguins which live in cold climates are well equipped to cut the losses down to a minimum. Blubber, consisting of oils extracted from the rich planktonic food, is a bad conductor of heat, and so a thick layer just below the skin helps to insulate the body; in species like the emperor penguin which has to withstand very low temperatures during the course of its breeding season, up to one-third of the body weight may be blubber, which acts not only as a heat-conserving coat but also as an energy store.

Feathers also play a vital role in keeping penguins warm. An emperor penguin has a dozen to the square centimetre and 84 per cent of the thermal insulation is due to the plumage. The effectiveness of the feathers is achieved by the trapping of a layer of air next to the skin – air being a very inefficient conducter of heat. Each one is quite stiff and turned over at the tip, and has a fluffy outgrowth called an aftershaft near to the base. When neatly reposed, the feathers form a covering which is particularly resistant to disturbance by wind, so that the skin is protected from icy blasts; furthermore, the down-like aftershafts join up, forming another insulating layer immediately next to the skin. The penguin's body, then, besides being packed in blubber is wrapped in 'eiderdown' and string vest.

Such formidable insulation entails some risk of the birds at times becoming overheated, a condition as dangerous for

19

them as growing too cold. At the height of the Antarctic 'day', when the air temperature may approach 0°C (32°F), adélie penguins may show signs of heat stress and sit with their feathers ruffled, allowing the insulating air layer next to the skin to break up, and some heat to leave the body.

The sub-tropical or tropical species, for whom the chances of becoming too warm are obviously greater, have a number of modifications which help them to keep cool. These include an interesting method of neutralizing the heat-conserving effect of the blubber layer. Blubber could be an embarrassment to an overheated penguin; but if the bird's body becomes too hot a mass of blood vessels in the skin become gorged with blood, bringing heat from within the body through the blubber to the surface, where it is dissipated. A similar system is found in the whales and seals. Antarctic and sub-Antarctic species also have feathered tarsi (shanks), but those living in warmer areas have bare shanks, undoubtedly

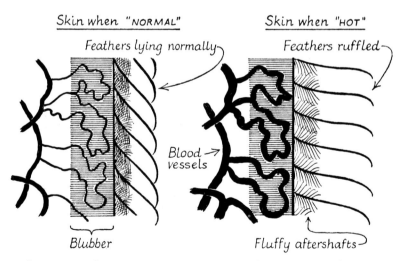

Section of Penguin skin to show how heat is lost from the surface by the swelling of blood vessels in the blubber and the opening of the feathers

connected with their role in dissipating heat.

Bare patches on the face, flippers and feet also act as radiators, so that superfluous heat generated by exercise or simply picked up as radiant energy from the sun can be lost from the body. Again, the bare facial surfaces of the *Spheniscus* penguins, and their flippers and feet, can be flushed with hot blood if the body temperature rises above its normal level, the heat consequently being transferred to the air.

Because of their very large surface area in relation to their bulk, the flippers are probably the most effective radiators: a penguin when relaxed, and neither too hot nor too cold, sits with its flippers held closely to its flanks, so that the cool air does not reach their warm undersurface; but should the bird become hot after exercising, it holds its flippers away from its body so that both their surfaces are exposed to the air, with a consequent increase in heat loss. African elephants use their ears in a similar way.

Dr Bernard Stonehouse, one of the pioneers of modern penguin research, found that in relation to its body size the erect-crested penguin from the Bounty and Antipodes islands to the south-east of New Zealand, has the largest flippers. It nests on bare rocks and needs a greater surface for losing heat than those which nest in cover, shielded from the sun. On the other hand, the magellanic penguin has relatively the smallest flipper, and this may be because it is one of a tropical group of penguins which has penetrated south, almost to a sub-Antarctic climate, and correspondingly needs to shed less heat.

Size also has an important bearing upon heat problems in animals. The heat capacity of a body depends upon its volume, but the speed at which heat can be lost to the surroundings depends not only on the heat gradient (i.e. the difference between the temperature of the body and the outside) but also on the surface area. A larger body will lose heat relatively less quickly than a smaller one of the same shape under similar conditions, because its volume will have increased relatively more than its surface area. There is therefore a definite advantage in being large, like an emperor penguin, when living in extremely cold conditions, and in being comparatively small when living in the tropics. Adélie penguins, which have to face the sub-zero temperatures of Antarctica, make up for their small size by having relatively long feathers, enabling them to hold a thicker layer of insulating air next to the skin.

Peruvian Penguin cooling itself by holding out its flippers and fluffing up its body feathers.

Apart from the emperors, penguins living today would appear Lilliputian if compared with some of the species found as fossils, which grew to a height of 1·5m (5ft) and must have weighed a few hundred kilograms (several hundred pounds). Their size leads one to expect that they lived in Antarctic conditions, but in fact they probably enjoyed a fairly temperate climate between eleven and twenty-five million years ago, in the Miocene period; the South Polar lands did not become heavily glaciated until the beginning of the Pleistocene era, about two million years ago. These man-sized birds may have had relatively less fluffy and shorter feathers, with larger flippers to act as radiators, than the birds we know today.

Let us now look at some of the structural features which have made penguins so successful.

As already mentioned, the evolution of feathers, together with the ability of birds to utilize energy at a high rate, made flight possible. However, flight is exacting; it demands the expenditure of far more energy than any other mode of progression and it also requires that such sense organs as eyes and the organs of balance in the middle ear should be highly developed to make possible quick alterations in muscular activity. Should a relatively heavy flying animal develop an uncontrollable stall, then it must crash, with probably fatal consequences; so the ability to correct immediately any tendency to stall is vital to birds – a momentary aberration or mistake may be the last one! Animals which always have their feet firmly planted on the ground are never confronted with such critical problems of stability and have never developed the powers to cope with them; early philosophers who thought that man could gain the freedom of the air merely by fixing wing-like structures to his arms clearly did not understand that his nervous equipment for flight did not match up to his genius for invention.

Birds are highly manœuvrable flying machines; consider a swallow as it hawks over a brook, flying in a determined course one moment, now twisting upwards and almost stalling, then abruptly plummetting and changing direction in its ceaseless pursuit of insects. But with aerial machines, manœuvrability and stability do not go together; the school-boy's paper dart is highly stable but it flies only in straight lines. Birds, with their ability to alter direction extremely

Royal penguins passing to and from their rookery on Macquarie Island (*Mary Gillham*)

quickly, more quickly than any aeroplane, are essentially unstable, and to keep airborne they must constantly adjust their trim. This involves continuous monitoring of their flight movements, information from their eyes and organs of balance being collected in order to assess whether adjustments are necessary and what these should be.

The monitoring goes on in a much-enlarged part of the mind brain, the cerebellum, which is in effect a most efficient computer for ensuring that the bird may remain in flight. The earliest fossil bird found had a cerebellum smaller than that of modern birds and so was probably a more stable and less agile flying animal than its descendants – a theory supported by the fact that it had a long stabilizing tail.

Flight is no less demanding of body structure than of the organs of balance and sight. The body of a bird is in essence a compromise between a framework designed to support flight and one which will allow movement on land. Because weight must be kept to a minimum for flight, the bones and muscles must be as light as possible.

The hind limbs and the attached muscles are used for walking, whereas the fore limbs and their muscles are used for flight; so there is a division of labour between the different parts of the body. Powerful muscles have been developed to actuate the wings and these are attached to rigid breastbone or sternum. The leg muscles are attached to a plate of bone, the pelvic girdle, around the hind region of the vertebral column, and again this is strengthened, because the legs take the impact of landing and also supply the force to launch the bird into the air. These two musculo-skeletal systems are fused into a rigid frame which will withstand the forces met while flying or landing. Birds to some extent make up for having a virtually immobile trunk by having a long and freely-moving neck – so that, for instance, all parts of the plumage may be preened.

This firm, boxed-in body structure means that birds which take to the water must propel themselves through it by some different method from that of most other underwater swimmers.

Many animals with backbones which live in water use a sinuous movement of the trunk or tail to get the necessary propulsive thrust from the surrounding fluid. In fish, sea-snakes and mammals such as otters, the lateral body waves can be seen moving from the front to the rear of the body, pushing the water backwards. Whales use a vertical sculling motion of the tail region to travel along at some speed. But for birds, the three obvious ways of swimming are to use the wings, the legs, or a combination of the two.

Different families of birds have specialized in using each of these methods. The ducks, divers and grebes, for example, all use the feet; accordingly their feet are fully webbed, or – in the grebes – their toes are furnished with large flattened lobes which spread out on the backward power stroke, presenting a large surface area of foot to thrust against the water. The lobes fold backwards, reducing resistance, as the leg is drawn forward into position for the next power stroke. The most efficient position for the legs is at the extreme rear, and so these birds have to remain fairly upright when walking on land, thus bringing their centre of gravity, which is set well forward, over their feet for balancing.

Most marine birds, including penguins, which hunt beneath the surface use their wings and literally fly under water. Interestingly, freshwater birds have not adopted this method: this may be because wings might become entangled in the vegetation common in fresh water; strongly webbed or lobate feet are more efficient here. In the sea, however, penguins and other birds have no monopoly in using their fore-limbs as sculls. A large number of fish, such as wrasses, progress by the delicate use of their forward or pectoral fins.

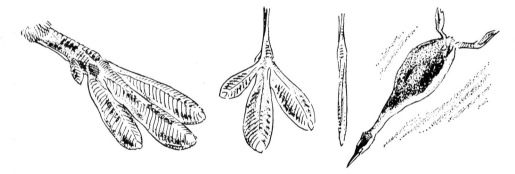

The foot of a Great crested Grebe showing the flattened leg and toes which spread out when thrust back and fold to a blade shape when brought forward.

The feet of two other water birds. The palmate foot of a duck, Mallard, (left and centre) and the totipalmate foot of the Shag, a sea bird.

Turtles, permanently girdled by a rigid shell, scull themselves in leisurely fashion through the oceans, although the hind limbs may be used to some extent. Among the marine mammals, sea lions may move their flippers in a vertical manner and literally fly through the water, although flexion of the body may also contribute some thrust.

As water is a fairly dense medium, a considerable amount of power is required for moving through it; this can be kept within reasonable limits by streamlining, which prevents the formation of swirls and eddies that would otherwise absorb valuable energy and hinder progression. The penguin's body is beautifully streamlined for swimming beneath the surface; indeed it approaches the ideal shape, with maximum width about one-third of the way from the front. When actively pursuing prey beneath the surface, the penguin's head is withdrawn into its shoulders and its feet pressed close to its body, which then assumes a clean, elongated, ovoid shape, offering least resistance to forward movement.

Similar streamlined shapes have been evolved quite independently by whales, dolphins and seals among the marine mammals, but the whales and dolphins probably have yet a further method of reducing turbulence. This was discovered when, on measuring the amount of power needed to drag a model dolphin through the water it turned out to be far more than the energy known to be expended by these animals when swimming at similar speeds. It seems that the skin and blubber may oscillate in response to turbulence, helping to quieten the swirling movement of the water and promoting a laminar or smooth flow over the skin. It remains to be seen whether the thick layer of oily feathers and the trapped air also act in this way in penguins.

Apart from the fact that drag may be reduced by streamlining, energy can also be most effectively used by swimming beneath the surface rather than on top of it. For example, at a speed of 9km per hour (5 knots) almost twice as much energy is needed to propel a body on the surface as is needed for underwater movement; this disparity increases to five times at 18km per hour (10 knots), ten times at 27km

Dolphins and Porpoises plunge in and out of the sea, enabling them to breathe without interrupting their forward progress.

They swim with a vertical sculling motion of the tail.

The superb streamlining of the Weddell Seal

The Turtle sculls itself through the water.

Sea Lion

Some of the many animals that have become adapted to a marine environment.

King Penguins "fly" underwater.

The Sei Whale, and others, use a vertical sculling motion of the tail region.

The Dipper is almost as much at home below as above water. They can swim, dive, fly and walk under water.

The Kingfisher's tiny feet are useless in its shallow dive for fish, so it uses its wings to leave the water.

The Dabchick closes its wings and swims with its broad flat toes.

The Velvet Scoter uses half open wings and feet.

The Black Guillemot "flies" underwater.

At the top are three freshwater birds and below three marine species, illustrating their various methods of underwater propulsion.

The Shag closes its wings and propels itself with its great paddle-like feet.

per hour (15 knots). Much of the wastage of energy occurring on the surface is caused by the production of bow and stern waves; these can readily be seen fanning out from ships ploughing their way through the sea. By often moving beneath the surface when at sea, penguins are able to reduce their muscular effort by a factor of between five and ten.

Penguins can and do sometimes swim on the surface, and in any case they have to come up regularly to breathe. But when travelling long distances to and from the feeding grounds, they do so by a method called 'porpoising'. As the name suggests, they swim like dolphins, plunging in and out of the sea, using their impetus to carry them out of the water only to plunge back a fraction of a second later with whirring flippers. This allows them to renew the air inside their lungs without interrupting their forward progression. Most penguins can keep up a steady speed of between 7 and 10km per hour (4–6 knots) plunging in and out of the sea, although underwater they can probably reach much higher speeds for short bursts. For an air-breathing marine animal, 'porpoising' is obviously an efficient way of moving around, and it has evolved independently not only in the penguins but also, of course, in the smaller whales (dolphins and porpoises).

Wing-propelled divers are found in all of the oceans, but whereas penguins and diving petrels are the predominant ones south of the Equator, to the north they are replaced by the twenty-two species of auks; these chunky little divers could be called the 'penguins' of the northern hemisphere and include such well-known species as puffins, guillemots and razorbills. The auks, with the exception of the extinct great

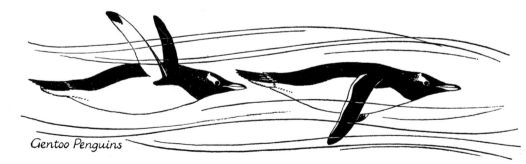

Gentoo Penguins

auk, can all fly and as Professor Robert Storer of the University of Michigan has pointed out, their ability to use the wings for both flight and swimming is closely connected with their size.

We perhaps take too much for granted that every species of animal differs in shape and size from all others. Bodily proportions and size have great survival significance, allowing each individual to live its particular way of life. Sparrows can no more soar on extended wings like buzzards than gulls can emulate penguins in underwater agility. Of course, much of this specialization hinges on the fact that body weight increases more rapidly than surface area with increasing dimensions – as previously mentioned when discussing the penguin's heat-conservation methods. If, for instance, the linear dimensions of a cube are doubled, the surface area increases four times but the weight becomes eight times the original. Since birds depend upon the surface area of their wings to support them in flight, as their bodies become larger their wings become proportionately less adequate to support the greater mass; and so wings tend to increase in relative size. A goshawk has larger wings in relation to its body size than has its smaller cousin, the sparrowhawk.

The auks have exploited all the ecological niches available to them – perhaps roughly the northern hemisphere equivalents of those taken by penguins in the southern hemisphere – evolving into species of varying sizes, from the smallest murrulets and dovekies to the larger guillemots or murres. But they are all relatively small when compared with the majority of penguins; their maximum attainable size has been

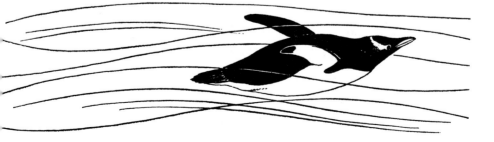

Some typical northern auks

Razorbill

Black Guillemot

Guillemot

Puffin

severely limited by their need to use their wings for flight *as well as* for underwater propulsion. (There is no large flightless diving bird in the northern hemisphere.) Wings must be relatively large if they are to gain enough lift for flying through the air, but for use in water, which is so much denser, a smaller, rigid structure is better; and the structure of a wing to be used in both media must be essentially a compromise.

For birds of the same shape, the larger individual will have to support a far greater weight on its wings, and will, therefore, tend to evolve proportionately larger ones. But for the heavier diving birds a correspondingly large wing would be unsuitably flexible and cumbersome if used under water. Wing size will accordingly be restricted to that capable of acting as an efficient underwater paddle; and the body size must not exceed that which can be borne aloft on these wings. Living species of auks have kept their powers of flight, and are clearly restricted in the size which they can attain; indeed razorbills and murres seem to have reached the maximum practicable limit for wing-propelled flying divers.

The smaller the birds the more closely will the optimum size of a wing for flight correspond with that of a wing (or flipper) for swimming; indeed, the 15–20cm (6–8in) long dovekies and the murrulets moult their primary and secondary wing feathers one at a time, because if all of them were shed at once, as in the other auks, the quill-less wing would be too small to be an effective paddle.

Once flight has been given up, then there is no limit on size. Resistance when swimming through the water will vary with the cross-sectional area of the bird – the area which meets the water head-on. This varies in the same proportion as the wing area, with the linear dimensions of the bird, and so increasing size involves only a small increase in wing dimensions, to provide the necessary extra power for swimming. Emperor penguins weigh nearly twice as much as king penguins, but their flippers are almost the same size. Similarly, the 75cm (30in) long extinct great auk was considerably larger than a razorbill (40cm/16in), but had wings

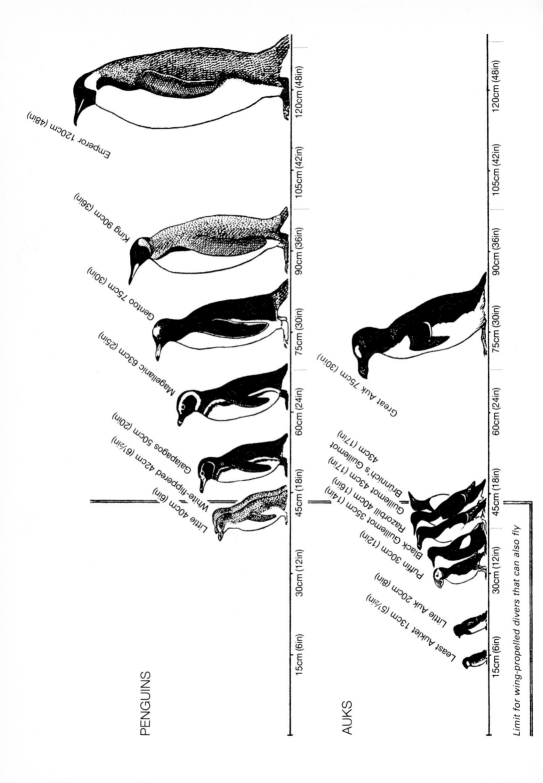

PENGUINS

Emperor 120cm (48in)
King 90cm (36in)
Gentoo 75cm (30in)
Magellanic 63cm (25in)
Galapagos 50cm (20in)
White-flippered 42cm (6½in)
Little 40cm (6in)

AUKS

Great Auk 75cm (30in)
Brünnich's Guillemot 43cm (17in)
Guillemot 43cm (17in)
Razorbill 40cm (16in)
Black Guillemot 35cm (14in)
Puffin 30cm (12in)
Little Auk 20cm (8in)
Least Auklet 13cm (5½in)

Limit for wing-propelled divers that can also fly

15cm (6in)   30cm (12in)   45cm (18in)   60cm (24in)   75cm (30in)   90cm (36in)   105cm (42in)   120cm (48in)

15cm (6in)   30cm (12in)   45cm (18in)   60cm (24in)   75cm (30in)   90cm (36in)   105cm (42in)   120cm (48in)

of similar size because it used them only for underwater flight. There has been no such limitation on the body size of penguins; indeed, the smallest species just overlap the largest auks in size. From the little penguin, weighing 2–3kg (4–6lb), to the other end of the scale, the emperor, weighing perhaps 40kg (90lb), there is a twenty-fold range in size: this could not have been attained had penguins retained their powers of flight.

Of course, there are advantages that accompany an increase in size; the amount of food required is relatively less under similar conditions, and so a larger animal is in biological terms a cheaper one to keep alive, bulk for bulk. Even so there are limits, and these may change according to the circumstances at any given period of time; giant penguins were not able to survive beyond the Miocene period for reasons that may never be known. Nevertheless, the present-day emperor penguin is able to maintain its body heat the more easily in Antarctica because of its large size.

The legs of penguins are not used for propulsion but they do help to steer, acting as rudders, and for this are well-placed at the rear of the body. Penguins, like the foot-propelled divers, must accordingly adopt an upright posture on land, an attitude which is partly responsible for their popularity: indeed, any animal which adopts a fairly vertical and thus humanoid stance is almost bound to endear itself to humans – as owls, bears, koalas and kangaroos have done.

When compared with the wings of other birds, the penguin's flipper is much modified for its use underwater. The wing bones are broadened and flattened to take the thrust of the water as the flipper beats against it; there are no elongated wing feathers, which would prove too flexible for underwater use, the surface of the flipper being covered with rows of scale-like feathers, the sole remains of the wing plumage. The wrist and elbow joints are fused for the sake of rigidity, with the result that the flipper cannot be folded when at rest but remains extended like an arm.

Movement at the shoulder joint is also partly restricted. As sea lions are nicely designed for balancing balls on their noses

Emperor
Penguin's
flipper

without undue difficulty, penguins seem to be always offering a friendly handshake, human-style; press or television coverage of a dignitary visiting a zoo will frequently show him grasping an extended flipper – the penguin remaining placidly unimpressed. Anyway, the two penguin characteristics which have near-universal appeal to humans are both inherent parts of the birds' elegant design ·for underwater swimming.

Penguins are superbly built for diving. Their performance, like that of any marine bird and mammal, depends upon how long they can hold their breath and keep warm, and the extent to which they can withstand the effects of water pressure. Much of the mystery about what happens when penguins disappear out of sight has in recent years been dispelled by radio tracking and by fitting them with automatic depth recorders which can be deciphered when the birds return to their nest sites. Data collected by scientists revealed that some species tend to be short and shallow divers, whereas others habitually hunt at depth, although the division between the two is a little blurred. The differences are partly related to diet and size, because large air-breathing creatures have an inherently greater diving capacity.

Gentoo penguins studied on South Georgia tended to dive to an average depth of 25m (81ft), although a considerable number of sorties were in excess of 80m (261ft). Chinstraps can reach depths of 70m (228ft) but the overwhelming majority of the dives recorded (90 per cent) are less than 45m (147ft), and 40 per cent are less than 10m (33ft), taking between 20 and 30 seconds. The jackass penguin on the other hand is another 'shallow' diver but tends to stay down for about 2½ minutes. The former species thrives on krill which are caught at night when the shrimps are swarming close to the surface. Therefore, there seems little need for krill eaters to expend energy unnecessarily by making deep hunting trips because they can make a comfortable living by undertaking short and relatively shallow forays. However, fast and wary mid-water squid and fish are the preferred prey of the king and emperor penguins. Not surprisingly, the emperor is the champion diver, holding the record duration, 18 minutes, and the depth record, 265m (867ft). However, the everyday performance may be a little less impressive. The average submergence is for about 2·4 minutes. More detailed information is available for the smaller king penguins. Three nesting at Schlieper Bay, South Georgia were closely monitored when they went to sea on a feeding trip. They were away between four and eight days and together logged 2,595 dives – daily averaging 144 per bird. Over half of the dives were greater than 50m (162ft) and two were deeper than 240m (783ft), which is a body crushing depth for any animal that takes down its own air supply. Predictably, seals and whales leave penguins standing in the diving stakes. Seals may regularly reach 300m (980ft), the record going to the Weddell seal, the world's most southerly mammal, which is known to dive to 600m (1,960ft) in McMurdo Sound, remaining underwater for over an hour. Even this pales by comparison with the performance of sperm whales, one of which in 1955 caught its jaw in a submarine cable lying in 1,134m (3,700ft) off the west coast of South America. However there is circumstantial evidence that they can reach depths well in excess of 3,000m (9,800ft)! By comparison, human skin divers rarely go deeper than 35m (115ft); sponge and oyster collectors treat this as their limit, but it is only equivalent to a 'shallow' dive for most penguins.

Water pressure has been one of the moulding forces on the evolution of the penguin's anatomy. Air is compressible and the volume of air taken down in the lungs and air sacs is reduced by 50 per cent with each 10m (33ft) descent below the surface. The interior of the air pipe (trachea) which travels from the back of the throat to the lungs is divided by a cartilaginous partition, which may prevent the walls from collapsing when the bird is swimming deeply. This feature is shared by seals and dugongs. There is also evidence that the windpipe can be expanded and contracted like a concertina by special muscles, a process which may aid the circulation of air between the lungs and the air sacs at the base of the neck (interclavicular air sacs). The air can therefore be wafted

37

backwards and forwards against the highly vascular lung surface, thus enhancing the absorption of oxygen. Although there appear to be no figures for penguins, diving mammals can probably utilize over 50 per cent of the oxygen from their lungs, whereas we humans do well to recover 25 per cent.

The penguin's physiology is even further adapted to make the best use of the air in the lungs and air sacs. An adélie penguin 'burns' 100cc (6cu in) of oxygen each minute when it is on the surface. If this rate was maintained during a dive, it would give the bird a theoretical underwater duration of between two and three minutes. But after it submerges, the heart slows down from 100 beats per minutes to 20. A similar phenomenon is displayed by seals and whales. In these mammals the reflex slowing of the heart is accompanied by a preferential shunting of the blood to the brain, while the rest of the body obtains its sustenance from glycogen deposited in the muscles and largely metabolized without oxygen. Even so, the muscles of these diving creatures and birds in general carry a great deal of oxygen loosely attached to myoglobin, a respiratory pigment similar to haemoglobin. Deep breathing on the surface saturates the myoglobin, which thus acts as a valuable oxygen store during the dive. Such adaptations enable diving animals to eke out their meagre supply of air and so sustain their underwater forays for as long as possible.

Taking down only one 'breathful' of air, these animals avoid 'the bends' (or decompression sickness) and nitrogen narcosis which plague scuba divers who rely upon com-pressed air delivered at ever-increasing pressure as they descend deeper and deeper. Unless great care is taken, the high concentration of nitrogen in the body generates a drunken-like state of euphoria, known as 'raptures of the deep', and too rapid a return to the surface might cause bubbles to materialize in the blood and joints, like taking the cap off a bottle of 'fizz'. Whales and seals largely avoid this by allowing their chests to collapse, forcing the residual air into parts of the respiratory tract which are not very vascular. Excessive nitrogen does not enter their bloodstream.

Penguins might suffer more discomfort through the loss of

body heat. The water pressure certainly squeezes the layer of insulating air from beneath the feathers, as witnessed by the trail of bubbles which diving penguins often leave behind them. It is therefore important for the submerged birds to score well in terms of catching food – after all, food is energy. It has been calculated that any of the species which feed on krill need to snatch one of these Euphausid shrimps on average every six seconds to satisfy both their own needs and those of their growing families. Kings and emperors with a penchant for meaty squid and fish need successful interception on only 10 per cent of the 865 or so dives undertaken on a feeding trip of several days' duration.

Penguins often have a number of stones in the crop; indeed 4·5kg (10lb) have been taken from the crop of an emperor. Although they may be used for macerating the food to facilitate digestion, these stones may also be swallowed as ballast to reduce buoyancy and aid diving. Many diving birds, including penguins, possess solid bones and these also may help to keep their owners low in the water. The bones of most birds are hollow or are heavily sculptured to decrease their weight for flight.

The life of a hunter is beset with difficulties, and many carnivorous creatures have evolved elaborate behavioural and structural adaptations to enhance their chances of success. Once beneath the surface of the sea, a penguin needs to see its prey. To do so, it must have eyes specially designed to cope with the problems of sub-aquatic vision. Anyone who has attempted to see underwater without the use of goggles knows that eyes whose optics are engineered to work in air only resolve blurred and relatively colourless images when immersed. Penguins possess underwater vision as well as good top-side sight. The essence of the problem faced by any diving bird, and ourselves for that matter, is that when the eyes are bathed in water, the power of the cornea (the clear, usually curved window at the front of the eye which bends light as a lens) is reduced, and the image finally resolved by the eye's crystalline lens is brought to a focus way behind the retina. Thus, underwater, we humans become very long-

Gannets

sighted and our vision loses all of its detail. Diving birds like cormorants solve the difficulty by powerful accommodating muscles which squeeze the bungy lens into a very curved shape, forcing it to bulge out through the iris, thereby 'pulling' the image forward onto the retina. But penguins have adopted a different optical strategy. Curiously, their corneas are uniquely almost flat, leaving the job of focussing almost entirely to the lens. Now in air, the penguin's relaxed or unaccommodated eye is short-sighted – that is, the image is focussed well in front of the light-sensitive retina. However, when the bird dives, the plane of focus moves back onto the retina, thereby restoring the visual acuity so vital for sub-aquatic hunting.

With its eye optics primarily designed for underwater, is a penguin hopelessly myopic in air? Apparently not. It may be able to flatten its lenses and reduce the size of the pupils to about a millimetre in diameter; the eyes are thus converted into pin-hole cameras forming detailed images onto the retinas. But there is more; penguins possess a degree of binocular vision in air comparable to an owl's, although this drops markedly when the birds look underwater.

Penguins are also able to make best use of what colour is present beneath the surface of the sea. The problem is that water acts like a filter, daylight becoming progressively 'bluer' with increasing depth. When examined, the cone receptors in the retinas of penguins display maximum sensitivity to violet, blue, and green light. This means that these birds can discriminate very finely between the hues in those parts of the spectrum. There is even a possibility that penguins can perceive ultra violet, although they are less sensitive to the red end of the spectrum which is very rapidly absorbed by the sea. So a penguin's view of the underwater world is very similar to that of a marine fish – clearly focussed and

Birds that spend much of their time on the water have evolved specific recognition marks, chiefly on the head region (i.e. the part that shows above the waves). This diagram shows how different conventions have been developed independently in both penguins and other birds.

40

Slavonian Grebe

Tufted Puffin

Guillemot

Razorbill

Red-throated Diver

Black-throated Diver

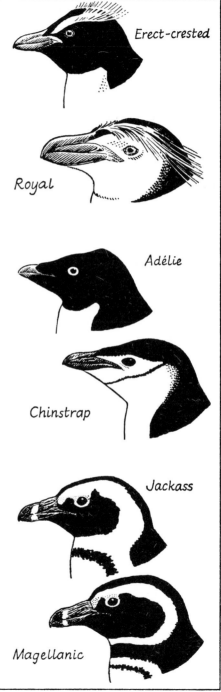

Erect-crested

Royal

Adélie

Chinstrap

Jackass

Magellanic

with a colour sensitivity well matched to the spectral proper-
ties of the medium through which it swims.

The next problem to be faced by a penguin is how to
approach its prey within striking distance without being seen
itself. Blending into the background is a widespread device
among hunters. Angler fishes, with a modified part of their
dorsal fin, lure unwary prey into their open mouth;
chameleons are able to intercept insect prey more easily by a
combination of stealthy behaviour and camouflage. Dazzling
white birds like adult gannets and most species of gulls are,
on the contrary, very conspicuous when viewed from above
the sea. It has been suggested that the plumage allows the
individuals to keep in visual contact when foraging several
miles apart; as soon as one starts feeding, perhaps plunge-
diving into a shoal of mackerel, then it attracts a host of
other birds to the food supply. What advantage this brings to
the individual who originally came upon the food supply is
not clear, unless the rapacious flock somehow disperse the
shoal and make feeding easier.

It has been pointed out, however, by Dr Graham Phillips, a
zoologist working at Oxford, that a bird with white
underparts flying over the sea, or indeed swimming, is less
easily seen by fish than one with dark plumage. The white
underparts of so many fish-eating seabirds may therefore be
an adaptation for catching fish by plunge-diving, improving
the bird's chances of not startling the prey. Penguins may be
partly camouflaged by their white-bellies and the white
under-surfaces of their flippers. If the white underparts are
not easily seen by fish, they will also be less likely to attract
lurking killer whales and leopard seals, both penguin killers.

Having come to within striking range of the prey, the
penguin has efficient weapons to dispatch it. Its spiny tongue,
helped by powerful mandibles, can gain purchase on the
slippery fish, crustaceans, or squid on which it feeds, and it
can swallow without fear of drowning. Macaroni penguins
may indeed use their bills to stun their prey before attempting
to eat it; the sharp, cleft-shaped bill of magellan and peruvian
penguins could inflict mortal wounds on any fish.

Penguins, particularly those that live in the krill-laden waters surrounding Antarctica, eat a lot of crustacean food, which poses a number of problems because, unlike fish, it contains a large quantity of salt; the salt concentration in crustaceans in fact resembles that of sea water, although the composition is slightly different. Sea birds have no access to fresh water to wash excess salt out of their bodies via the kidneys. The kidneys of birds and mammals can only excrete salt in small quantities, indeed in concentrations only about one-third of that of sea water; so if sea water is used to quench the thirst, in order to excrete the extra load of sodium chloride taken in, water will have to be withdrawn from the tissues to expel it. The net result of this will be dehydration.

Sea birds have therefore evolved special glands situated in front of and above the orbit (lateral nasal glands), which are able to extract a highly concentrated solution of salt from the blood; the excreted fluid is indeed far more saline than sea water. This solution is passed down ducts and finally expelled from the nose, where droplets often collect at the tip of the bill and are shaken off. All birds, like penguins, gulls, cormorants and 'tubenoses' (albatrosses, shearwaters, petrels), which possess nasal glands can therefore drink sea water. It was thought that penguins in captivity needed to have their diet of fish supplemented with extra rations of salt in order to make good the loss through the nasal glands. However, as these glands only work in response to any increased salt load in the blood, this practice is unnecessary and no longer followed in zoos; the glands merely become defunct.

We have now dealt with the penguin as a bird which is superbly designed as an underwater predator and one which has sacrificed the powers of flight to gain perfection in sub-aquatic swimming. It has also been shown how other basic avian characteristics have, to some extent, become modified for the penguin's specialized existence. Now let us follow penguins on their journey through life.

2 · Courtship and Nest-making

It is ironical that so much of our information on penguins is about their life on the land – for these birds spend perhaps as much as two-thirds of their time at sea. What we do know about their life and dispersal at sea after they leave the breeding sites is largely the result of sightings from ships.

On the whole penguins are probably not great travellers at sea, tending to disperse in small parties from their rookeries to feed in the nearby coastal waters. The magellan and peruvian penguins, for example, feed in the rich waters of the Humboldt current, together with myriads of other sea birds which produce guano chiefly on the west coast of South America. South Africa's jackass penguin exploits the sardines and pilchards living just off the coast, and parties of these birds can be seen 30km (20 miles) out to sea. Parties of little penguins are often observed on the edge of the Australian continental shelf. Although many of these birds may not move vast distances from their rookeries, over 8,000 chicks have been ringed, and the analysis of 200 recoveries reveal that some may disperse 1,000km (620 miles) or more from their natal colonies. The main breeding area of the chinstrap penguin extends from Peter First Island (longitude 90° W) eastwards to Bouvet Island (just east of 0°) although there are breeding outposts on Kerguelen and the Balleny Islands. Outside the breeding season, chinstraps have been observed as far north as Macquarie Island and Port Stanley in the Falkland Islands. There is, then, a fairly wide, almost circumpolar, dispersal of this species, often in the autumn and winter, and some individuals do go north of the Antarctic Convergence, a boundary in the southern oceans marking a sudden change of sea temperature (see Chapter 4).

Young penguins may be more widely scattered by the currents than the adults; immature emperor penguins have a more northerly range than the adults, and may even penetrate the southern temperate regions and turn up in Tierra del Fuego. However, most adélie and emperor penguins spend their lives within the Antarctic circle, and when not pre-occupied with breeding are to be found among the pack ice; if emperors breed every year, then the mature individuals have a respite from rookery life only from mid-January to mid-March, and their oceanic wanderings will be correspondingly limited. After their pre-nuptial moult, the more sub-Antarctic king penguins spend two to three weeks at sea not far from the coast, fattening up for the breeding season which starts in September and October. Macaroni and rockhopper penguins, however, may make regular northerly migrations from their rookery sites, and this may be correlated with a corresponding movement of their food.

It is perhaps surprising that penguins, which are as supremely adapted to life in water as albatrosses are to soaring in the trade winds over the oceans, are tied to the land when breeding. The reason is that all birds have inherited a breeding system which probably has not altered in its bare essentials since feathers started to evolve in a group of bipedal reptiles some two hundred million years ago: the eggs are laid in a nest and incubated, and the young attended by one or both parents until they can care for themselves. The eggs are placed in some kind of structure and this must be placed on land for support. The aquatic grebes do build floating nests,

45

Gentoo penguins nesting showing their proximity to vegetation (*John Warham*)

but then they live in freshwater lakes and ponds, where wave formation would not normally be severe enough to upset or disintegrate them. The building of floating nests in marine habitats would probably not be of much survival value, and sea birds accordingly have not developed them.

The kind of places where rookeries are sited vary tremendously between species. Sea caves may be used by the galapagos and peruvian species, although the latter will burrow into guano beds on islands off the South American coast. The peruvian, magellanic and South African jackass penguins are all really burrow-nesters, but unfortunately much of the top-soil has been removed from areas where the jackass breeds, and man has taken away most of the fossilized guano in which the peruvian penguins used to excavate their nests. Peruvian penguin eggs perhaps 10,000 years old have been found in opencast guano mines. This mass of compacted and dried-out sea-bird droppings is rich in minerals and an excellent fertilizer, and so millions of tonness have been removed, an industry being set up to harvest each year's accumulation from the bird colonies. As the layer over the bare rock is not allowed to grow thick enough for the fossorial – burrowing – penguins to dig into, many must now nest on the surface in shallow depressions, or in caves.

Rockhopper and royal penguins and some of the other crested species may burrow through tussock grass, making avenues to sites several hundred yards away from the sea; on Tristan da Cunha the annual passage of rockhoppers has worn lava flows smooth. On Macquarie Island the rock-hoppers stake out areas among the tussock grass for their large colonies, tending to overlap the smaller groups of royal penguins which occupy the more open and level areas between boulders. By and large, many of the sub-Antarctic species nest fairly close to the sea. Gentoo rookeries are sometimes situated in ice-free rocky areas, and as this species apparently needs a growth of vegetation round the sites, these are changed every two or three years to allow them to recover from the incessant trampling. Further south, the gentoo is replaced by chinstrap and adélie penguins respectively.

47

Though the rookeries are generally fairly near the sea, they may be far removed from the nearest free water, particularly during the winter and early spring when the breeding season is starting for the adélie and the emperor. As the winter closes in, much of the sea surrounding Antarctica freezes over for several hundreds of miles, but with the coming of summer the ice disperses, pieces of the ice shelves break off and channels of sea then open the way southwards to the breeding sites. Emperor penguins nest on ice, so they in particular must place their rookeries far enough from the water not to be endangered by the breaking up and melting of the ice in the height of the Antarctic summer, but not so far as to compel a long journey to the open sea to collect food for the chicks when they arrive. The emperor penguin is perhaps the only species of bird which never sets a foot on the land, passing its entire life at sea or on Antarctic ice shelves.

The adélie and emperor penguins are the most accomplished overland travellers. During September–October, the time when members of the former species start to move southwards, the traditional rookery sites are often 50–60km (30–40 miles) from the edge of the sea ice; the rookery site in the Hope Bay colony at the tip of the Antarctic peninsula, indeed, has been reckoned to be about 320km (200 miles) away from the sea. Although this seems exceptional, many adélie penguins must walk or toboggan about 50 or 60km (30 or 40 miles) over rough sea ice to gain their nest sites. From the published figures there seems to be a relationship between

Rockhoppers in tussock grass.

Adélie penguins passing to and from their rookery. The dirty ones are coming from the rookery (*Alfred Saunders*)

the size of the rookeries and their distance from the edge of the sea in October. Several hundred thousand adélie penguins nest around Ross Island and off Cape Crozier where the spring migration may be of no great length – perhaps only 2·5km (1½ miles) – because of the early dispersal of ice in the south-west corner of the Ross Sea; whereas a colony in Marguerite Bay in Western Antarctica contains only 600–800 pairs, and is about 95km (60 miles) from the sea in the early spring. The most southerly rookery is at Cape Royds, just in front of Sir Ernest Shackleton's hut on Ross Island where 1,250 pairs of adélies nest. Although only 1,450km (900 miles) from the South Pole, snow petrels nest a little further south and Antarctic skuas no doubt forage wherever humans leave something to scavenge upon.

Adélies may nest at considerable heights above sea level. On Philip Island, Wilson, the explorer, found a rookery of well over 200,000 of these birds and some were nesting 300m (1,000ft) above sea level. Emperor penguins, too, may have to toboggan or walk about 95km (60 miles) over stable sea ice in sub-zero temperatures to reach their rookeries. Tracks probably belonging to an emperor have been found 299km (186 miles) from the nearest open sea at 77° 30′ S, 98° 54′ W, heading east of south in a remarkably true course; but the record is probably held by a chinstrap, whose toboggan tracks were discovered 400km (250 miles) from the nearest known sea. Adélies and emperors must possess a creditable degree of homing ability, particularly as the nature of the terrain makes landmarks of limited use and it is also thought that penguins are slightly short-sighted in air.

Richard Penney and Professor John Emlen have investigated the homing ability of adélie penguins. Dr Penney removed five unsuccessful breeding males from Wilkes Station by air and released them at McMurdo, some 3,800km (2,360 miles) from their rookery. At least two and probably three individuals arrived, ten months later, at their place of capture so they must have travelled at an average speed of 13km (8 miles) per day towards base during those ten months. This proved that displaced birds can find their way back home, but further studies were designed to find out exactly what kind of clues they used. Of course, penguins are ideal subjects for these kind of homing studies because their inability to fly makes them easy to follow after their release on land; also, as the Antarctic ice cap is practically featureless, it is easy to test whether penguins are using celestial features for orientation in much the same way as mariners do with sophisticated sextants. Anyway, adélies were transported chiefly from Cape Crozier, on the edge of the Ross Sea, and released at points on Victoria Land, Marie Byrd Land and the Ross Ice Shelf (see map on page 208/9), so that some birds were displaced up to 1,500km (930 miles) from their rookery. After their release, the penguins moved off in a NNE direction towards the coast. This orientation was quite consistent under certain conditions, although it was obvious that the birds were not homing directly to the rookery.

Adherence to a fixed departure direction, with apparent disregard of the home direction, is known as a 'nonsense orientation' and has been noted in many other kinds of birds, such as pigeons, terns and ducks; and for penguins this nonsense orientation must have a high survival value. Birds displaced inland will always find their way back to the sea, and therefore to the feeding grounds, and Richard Penney noticed that those birds which returned to the rookery the

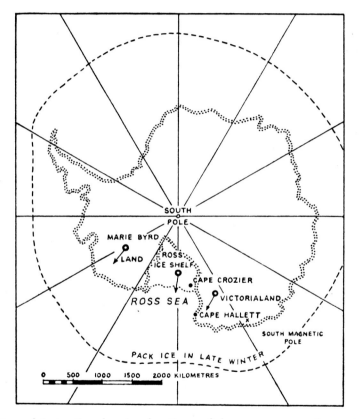

Map of Antarctica showing locations of the two sources of experimental birds and the three release sites. Mean departure direction of Cape Crozier birds released under good sun are indicated by an arrow at each release site.

same season looked healthy and well fed. On reaching the sea, the birds presumably re-orientate and then swim round the coast until they reach their home base. The fact that all the experimental birds, released one at a time, moved off in the same direction implies that they must have been able to assess their bearings correctly.

It seems from Penney's and Emlen's work that the penguins use the sun as their main clue, because under cloudy conditions they dispersed randomly (see figure), whereas as soon as the sun appeared they regained their NNE course. To use the sun as a compass bearing, the birds must also have to take into account the time of day as it moves across the sky – to compensate for its changing azimuth. In Antarctica during the summer the sun's course does not dip below the horizon

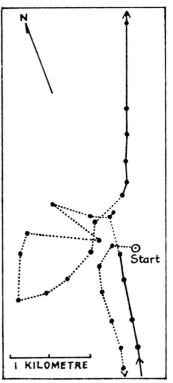

Course taken by an adélie penguin. The dots represent the plotted positions at 5 minute intervals. Those joined by a dotted line represent the course taken under a cloud covered sky. The black line shows its progress when the sun emerges from the cloud cover, and the bird is then able to orientate.

52

and it moves through an arc of approximately 15° each hour (360° a day); so it is in the NNE position only once during the day time. Because the earth is tilted on its axis the apparent course taken by the sun is elliptical, and therefore its apparent angular movement varies: 15° per hour is only an average figure. If penguins are to orient themselves accurately their sense of timing must allow for this. Should they fail to do so, they would tend to head slightly east of the mean direction (NNE) before midday, and west of it in the afternoon. In the experiment, twenty-eight birds released in the morning made a 10° shift to the east, and twenty-three birds released during the afternoon made a 12° shift to the west! Clearly they have no compensation device to correct for the eccentric path taken by the sun in these latitudes.

So, like many other animals, penguins must have an inherent sense of timing, a 'biological clock' which can be used for solar navigation. Although they have a 'nonsense orientation' of NNE, this course is only rigidly held when the birds are lost. As they are capable of navigating by the sun they may be guided by it on their long treks to the rookeries at the beginning of the breeding season, in the same way as other migrating birds use the stars and sun in their migrational flights.

The differences between the rookery sites selected by the two low Antarctic species are interesting. The small adélies, vulnerable to being smothered in snowdrifts which accumulate in sheltered hollows, usually nest on rocky slopes, exposed to the wind. But of the twenty-six known colonies of emperors, totalling 200,000 pairs, all but two are located on fast sea-ice (i.e. it does not melt annually) and are fairly well sheltered. The males often have to face blizzards in which the temperature may drop as low as −50°C (−60°F), and so conserving heat has great survival value. Under these conditions the birds huddle in order to keep warm (as described later in the chapter) and this behaviour is more effective if carried out on a flat surface, such as the ice offers and the rocky areas do not. Some emperor rookeries are situated in the lee of ice cliffs which give the birds some

Emperor penguin rookery, showing the absence of any degree of regular spacing and tolerance of bodily contact between individuals (*Jean Prévost, Expéditions Polaires Françaises*)

degree of shelter. At the same time the birds must have access to open water when the young are ready to leave.

The birds tend to remain faithful to their own rookeries and return year after year; in fact one of the first scientific ringing experiments was carried out in Antarctica on adélie penguins. On 12 January 1909, L. Gain, a member of the second French Antarctic Expedition, placed green celluloid bands on forty gentoos, and fifty adult and seventy-five young adélies, and proved conclusively that the adults at least returned to the same rookery in subsequent years. In a later ringing experiment, by Richard Penney, it was estimated that only about 1·5 per cent of adult adélie penguins ever change from one rookery to another. And each season the birds return to breed in their own territory within the rookery. Although an adélie rookery may look as though it consists of a homogeneous mass of birds it nevertheless has an underlying structure; each may contain a large number of discrete groups of pair territories, forming smaller societies or neighbourhoods within a teeming city. It has been estimated that only about 2·3 per cent of adélies change from one neighbourhood to another. So it is with little penguins which show amazing loyalty to one particular rookery.

The first birds to arrive at the rookeries are the males, who come to establish territories and nest sites in preparation for the females. Possession of a territory is a prerequisite for successful breeding for all penguins except emperors which have no nest and shuffle around with their eggs. As every bird is boss within his own private area around the nest site, the activities associated with reproduction can be carried out with the minimum of interference. The site may have to be fought for, and will certainly have to be defended. Fighting is common in the breeding season in adélie, rockhopper and yellow-eyed penguins, much of it precipitated by newcomers, birds which have not bred before, attempting to gain a place in the rookery. They may be successful in obtaining a peripheral nest site, but among adélie penguins latecomers tend not to breed. Gaining a place in the rookery does not necessarily guarantee a mate either, as in yellow-eyed

(*opposite*) Chicks and adult adélie penguins at a colony on Torgeson Island (*Wolfgang Kaehler*)

(*overleaf*) The penguin family showing associated species and comparative sizes (*Robert Gillmor*)

1   Emperor penguin *Aptenodytes forsteri*
2   King penguin *Aptenodytes patagonicus*
3   Fiordland crested penguin *Eudyptes pachyrhynchus*
4   Erect-crested penguin *Eudyptes sclateri*
5   Rockhopper penguin *Eudyptes chrysocome*
6   Macaroni penguin *Eudyptes chrysolophus*
7   Royal penguin *Eudyptes schlegeli*
8   Snares island penguin *Eudyptes robustus*
9   Adélie penguin *Pygoscelis adeliae*
10 Gentoo penguin *Pygoscelis papua*
11 Chinstrap penguin *Pygoscelis antarctica*
12 Little penguin *Eudyptula minor*
13 White-flippered penguin *Eudyptula (minor) albosignata*
14 Yellow-eyed penguin *Megadyptes antipodes*
15 Magellanic penguin *Spheniscus magellanicus*
16 Jackass penguin *Spheniscus demersus*
17 Peruvian penguin *Spheniscus humboldti*
18 Galapagos penguin *Spheniscus mendiculus*

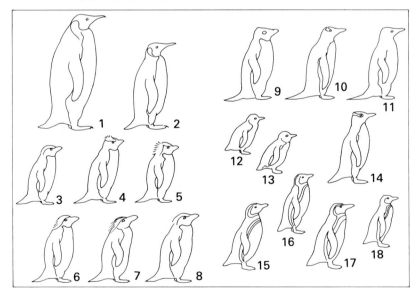

penguins there may be more males than females, the cause underlying innumerable quarrels.

At this time of the year, most kinds of penguins become transformed into sexually active, intensely social and yet hugely quarrelsome creatures. With over a million birds jostling together in the largest rookeries, widespread chaos and bloodshed is avoided through the performance of much ritual. The penguins behavioural repertoire is thus extended during the nesting season to include a bevy of postures and calls which help to smooth the relationships between the members of these seabird cities. These displays facilitate the establishment of pieces of freehold with the minimum amount of fuss, assist in advertising a penguin's status (i.e. its sex, whether it is paired or not), securing the cooperation of a mate in the act of copulation, and in reinforcing the pair bond.

Penguins are nothing if not garrulous. Apart from their bugle-like contact calls which enable the birds to keep in touch with each other, and aggressive grunting, they are blessed with the capacity to sing. However, their songs are not in the same class as the mellifluous tones uttered from the throats of nightingales and mockingbirds. A penguin's best tune is a series of coarse trumpet-like honks. However, scientists, such as Dr Pierre Jouventin, who have laboured hard to decipher the language of these birds are nevertheless convinced that these lugubrious vocalizations are every bit as meaningful to lovelorn penguins as the songbird's tuneful utterances. Apart from helping a cock penguin to establish its territory and summon a mate, the song may well be a crucial means of assisting the birds to identify each other. Experiments carried out in the rookeries confirm this assertion. For

(*above*) The most truly antarctic of all birds: a huddle of six-week-old emperor penguin chicks on the Brunt Ice Shelf, Antarctica (*Doug Allan, Oxford Scientific Films*)

(*below*) Nine-month-old king penguin chicks with adults, South Georgia (*Doug Allan, Oxford Scientific Films*)

Pair of chinstrap penguins head-waving at their nest site (*Alfred Saunders/Frank Lane Picture Agency*)

instance, paired emperors which have no nest or fixed territory and which breed on sea-ice bereft of landmarks keep close to each other during the period preceding egg laying. If the birds are separated so that they lose sight of each other, they are curiously unable to recognize each other – other than by voice. Just after the egg is laid, the mated couple often engage in an antiphonal duet, perhaps ensuring that each remembers its partner's voice prior to leaving the rookery. Since the largest emperor colonies contain 50,000 milling adults, all looking alike, it is not surprising that the birds need as much help as possible to locate their partners.

Most penguins sing during the course of showing them- selves off. Their displays tend to be variations on two basic themes. One involves the bird stretching itself up, throwing its head back and skypointing. The other is the antithesis and is based upon bowing. The relatively restricted spectrum of courtship displays (compared with gannets, boobies, and gulls) might be a consequence of the penguin's design for 'flying' through the water. For example, the rigidity of the shoulder joint and the blade-like flippers curtail movement of the forelimbs and thus the potential for signalling.

One display prominent in a rookery early in the breeding season is called the 'Ecstatic' and is found in all penguins with the exception of the emperor. In the adélie, it consists of a few preliminary movements of the head to one side, followed by a stretching of the neck so that head and bill point vertically upwards. The flippers are moved in a rhythmic way, while the chest is thrust outwards, the bird giving vent to a clamorous song. It reaches the climax as the head feathers are raised and the call changes to a braying sound. Adélies keep the bill shut, others open it.

Among adélies, the Ecstatic display is given chiefly by male birds which are not established or, more often, which are just asserting themselves in their territories. An adélie performing an Ecstatic display certainly catches the eye, even among a busy mass of birds. Its effect upon other birds is probably twofold: unpaired females are attracted, and males may be intimidated. It also seems to have a 'social facilitation' effect;

63

"Ecstatic" display in three species of penguin

Yellow-eyed

(After Richdale 1951)

Adélie

Chinstrap

that is, the display tends to be taken up by males in adjacent territories, thereby reinforcing the ownership of each patch.

By contrast, the emperor drops his head onto his chest, and this may be connected with the mechanics of his song production. The visual aspect of this species' display during the early part of the nesting season appears to be less important than in the related king penguin, the males of which are highly belligerent in defending their patches of ground.

Pair formation may be a more complex business in the king penguin, as it first involves the male in performing an Ecstatic display which attracts unmated hens, and when one arrives this is followed by a bout of antiphonal calling and head-flagging. The individuals spend some time looking at

Two displays of King Penguin during pair formation.

Ecstatic display.

The "advertisement walk", viewed from behind and from the side.

Emperor penguins displaying (G. *Harrow*)

each other, and then looking away, behaviour which in other birds has been related to appeasement and may be important in reducing any fear between the partners. Following this, the male thrusts his chest forward, arches his back, and with neck extended walks forward; if the female accepts she follows him. Bright patches of coloured feathers or the sudden exposure of conspicuous patterns are used often by birds to make displays visually more striking. This rarely applies to penguin displays, but in the 'advertisement walk' of the king penguin, the head makes a 90-degrees pendulum movement from side to side, so that the vivid orange ear-patches of the leading bird are alternately displayed to their full extent to the following one. These patches may help to elicit following behaviour, thus leading to pair formation.

The emperor penguin has markings similar to those of the king. Courtship among adélies is energetic and brings a daily weight loss of 73g (2½oz), an appreciable amount of fat in a bird weighing about 5·4kg (12lb) on arrival in the rookery.

When the hens arrive in the rookeries, then, they are met by males, all holding their own nest sites and displaying. The Ecstatic display may help to distinguish the males in the community; in most species the sexes look similar, although in little penguins the males may be distinguished by their thicker bills and larger white patches beneath the tail; rockhopper penguins also show a sex distinction in bill structure with the males having the deeper bill. Females tend to behave in a submissive manner, and may wander around from partner to partner, finally keeping with one male and copulating with him. What exactly determines the choice of mate is unknown. It was once suspected that penguins are already mated before they reach the rookeries, but this has not been substantiated by recent research. The late L. E. Richdale, the well-known penguin authority of New Zealand, found that yellow-eyed penguins tend to return to the nest site where they bred the year before, and to keep the same mate; indeed most of those that changed mates probably did so because of the death or disappearance of one of the partners.

Snares island penguins displaying (*John Warham*)

Richard Penney investigated nest site and partner tenacity in adélie penguins by ringing a large number of birds at Wilkes and following their marital history in subsequent breeding seasons. Of 282 pairs under surveillance, 139 reunited on their old nest sites, four moved and only twenty-nine of the pairs dissolved. In this sample, fourteen pairs failed to turn up and a hundred pairs were split by one or other of the mates failing to return. So 83 per cent of the pairs reunited in the following season if the original mate was at hand; the divorce rate was 17 per cent.

Dr. J. C. Coulson, working on kittiwakes, rather specialized cliff-nesting gulls, has demonstrated that pairs which have had an unproductive breeding season tend in the subsequent year to change partners more readily than those which have reared two or three young. It is therefore interesting that most of those adélie penguin adults which changed their group residence were females which had previously had an unsuccessful breeding season. Reunited pairs rarely changed their territories, and the four pairs which did so moved less than 2.7m (3yd) in a subsequent season. On the other hand, females whose previous mates failed to show themselves were far more vagrant than males similarly bereft. There are some interesting observations on the birds whose mates were late in arriving. Some of the females paired off with new mates, but quickly reverted to their previous one if he turned up within a few days.

In a recently reported study of little penguins which live in Victoria, P. Reilly and J. M. Cullen of Monash University were unable to confirm a relationship between unproductive breeding and divorce. An average of 18 per cent of the pairs split up each year irrespective of whether the individuals had had a good or bad previous season. The length of time a pair had been together did not seem to affect the likelihood of a separation either. The most faithful pair recorded, which had nested for eleven consecutive years was also consistent with a divorce rate of 18 per cent per year. However, birds with fresh partners tended to get down to the business of breeding a little earlier in the season. Divorced or widowed females with fresh mates laid about three weeks earlier than during their previous nesting season.

Study of the New Zealand yellow-eyed penguins shows that in any particular breeding season there is a divorce rate of 13–18 per cent among those pairs where both mates turned up, and this is comparable with that of the adélies and little penguins. In 58 per cent of the cases studied the pair bond lasted one year, in 39 per cent from two to six years, and in 3 per cent seven to thirteen years; one pair was observed to breed for thirteen consecutive years.

It has been thought that the general marital fidelity among penguins was due to an attachment of both partners to the nest site: as both male and female would tend to return to their breeding spot of the year before, they would automatically pair up again in successive seasons. The latest work on adélie penguins, however, indicates that although they do tend to assemble in the territories held in the previous year, there is also unquestionable evidence for individual recognition. Scientists who have worked with groups of penguins begin to discern individual differences after a time – so there is every reason to suppose that the penguins themselves may be able to recognize their fellows by visual characteristics. There are accounts of adélie penguins attempting to relieve incubating birds other than their mates, but the individual on the nest would give only a hostile reaction. Richard Penney found that he could gently lift neighbours off their eggs and swop them over, so that the relieving birds would go to their own territories but would be confronted with a strange mate.

Nesting Adélies

Northern Blue Penguin
(After photos in Kinsky 1960)

Mutual displays
in three species of penguin

Adélie

Rockhopper
(After Warham 1963)

Undue embarrassment was avoided because the mates reacted to each other's calls and located each other: so it seems that individual differences in the calls play an appreciable part in mutual recognition.

To rear young there must be a considerable amount of cooperation between the mates, in the act of copulation, in keeping the eggs warm, and in the lengthy process of supplying food and offering protection to the chicks until they can fend for themselves. Studies of animal behaviour show that adult birds tend to be mutually suspicious, their relations being often tinged, more or less, with rage and fear, particularly between strangers. Even mated birds may tend to be hostile or frightened of each other to some extent. Males and to some extent females have to assert themselves and be ready to threaten or fight off intruding individuals from their nest sites, which would otherwise be taken over by other more domineering birds – so aggressiveness during the breeding season has considerable survival value. Yet in the breeding season, mates who may have known each other only for a short time, and who are capable of being sexually aroused by any other individual in the community, must in the space of a few weeks get together and remain with each other in the territory, making their contribution to the next generation. In a sense, the mate is an intruder, but of a special kind who is tolerated. Any emotions which would hinder the shared and vital task must be held in check. The continuous displaying, which is so often characteristic of pair formation in penguins, may serve just this purpose of reassuring or appeasing the mate, reducing the domineering or apprehensive attitudes, thereby strengthening the pair bond and winning a degree of confidence which will allow the business of reproducing to proceed smoothly.

It is in this connection that the 'Mutual' displays of penguins are so important. Outwardly they are similar to the Ecstatic displays, but they are made by both birds. There are other smaller differences – for example, in the adélie the flippers are not vibrated and the bill is opened. Mutual displays are seen most frequently just before the eggs are laid,

Pair of Royal Penguins displaying.

Adélie penguins Mutually Displaying on their nest site. Note the elevated nape feathers, and the extensive feathering over the bill, helping to protect the small penguins from the cold (*F. C. Kinsky*)

and also during the nest-relief ritual; later in the breeding cycle the chicks may join in, and very often birds will break into Mutual displays after being disturbed or agitated; this would have the important function of reasserting ownership of nest sites, and re-establishing individual recognition of mates in a stylized way after the passing of some disruptive influence; no doubt conflicts and tensions are also worked off in the performance of these displays. Among the little penguins, Mutual displays take place inside the burrows, never in the open. Males and females stand beside each other with the flippers outstretched and vibrating, and both emit a wailing cry; their heads are held high, their beaks half open, and they repeatedly touch each other; at the height of each performance, the birds apparently slap each other on the back with their flippers.

Mutual displays are also well developed in other sea birds, such as gannets and albatrosses, where one member of the pair is away from the nest for some time searching for food. These elaborate performances no doubt help to reinforce recognition between the partners, as well as appeasing the hostile drive that is so necessary for protecting the nest site.

After pair formation, nest building starts. Penguins have to exploit whatever may be available to them as nest material, although the two largest, the emperor and king, dispense with this stage, as they incubate their single eggs between their abdomen and tarsi. The adélie piles up stones, but to find enough even of these can be a problem in the frozen wastes of deep Antarctica. A nest mound is first prepared, the birds lying on their bellies and scraping backwards with their feet; pebbles are then added to this until the cup is raised well clear of the ground, so that in the event of flooding the eggs are not chilled. The penguins' artfully unorthodox method of collecting their pebbles has much amused observers. Bernacchi wrote of the adélies at Cape Adare as being 'shameless thieves'.

> The thief slowly approaches the one he wishes to rob with a most creditable air of nonchalance and disinterestedness, and if, on getting closer, the other looks at him suspiciously, he will immediately gaze round almost child-like and bland, and appear to be admiring the scenery. The assumption of innocence is perfect; but no sooner does the other look in a different direction, than he will dart down on one of the pebbles of its nest and scamper away with it in his beak.

The prevalence of thieving was well illustrated by an

experiment performed by G. M. Levick, one of the early Antarctic biologists, and written up in his book in 1914. He presented different-coloured pebbles to adélies to test their colour preferences, and found they showed a predilection for red ones – which soon became distributed throughout the rookery. The incessant plundering of nest material among adélies is aggravated by their use of a nest-relief ceremony in which the returning bird sometimes brings a stone for the nest as a gesture of appeasement or greeting. Displays are often stylized and exaggerated forms of other activities, and this display is almost indistinguishable from ordinary nest building, although all observers feel that it has a symbolic and deeper meaning to the mate.

The period between the birds arriving at the rookery and the appearance of the first egg varies between species, being as long as seventy-two days in the sub-Antarctic gentoo penguin and as little as nineteen days in the rockhopper; for other species it is generally around twenty to thirty days. The sizes of the clutches are also variable, except with the emperor and king, which both lay only only egg. Some, such as macaroni penguins, may produce as many as three eggs, although the third one is often infertile. The macaroni's second egg is on average 71 per cent heavier than the first. Two eggs are usual for rockhoppers on Macquarie Island and probably elsewhere, but further north, on Tristan da Cunha, nests with three eggs are not uncommon and the islanders have reported clutches of four. The first egg laid by both the erect-crested penguin (whose normal clutch again appears to

Fiordland crested penguins at their nest site in a cold temperate rain forest (*John Warham*)

be two) and the rockhopper is much smaller than the second and may be crushed or kicked out of the nest before it hatches. This curious habit of discarding the first egg has also been reported from the royal penguins nesting on Macquarie Island. Deliberate ejection, noted for several of the crested species, was not confirmed by Ian Strange who recently made a thorough study of rockhoppers breeding in the Falkland Islands. On the contrary, the pairs he had under observation incubated all their eggs to hatching. If eggs are systematically removed by man, as many as ten may be laid by gentoo penguins, and adélies may lay a third after one of their normal two has been removed. Seventy-nine per cent of the adélie pairs studied by Dr Bernard Stonehouse at Cape Royds were incubating two eggs, the remaining 21 per cent had one, and the average in this particular rookery of adélie penguins turns out to be 1·85. A second egg would follow in, on an average, 3·1 days after the first, and a third one could be induced, on average, 3.4 days after the second. In this species the first egg is usually larger than succeeding ones.

Once the eggs have been laid usually the male penguins take over the first incubation stand, although at Signy Island one out of every sixty-three female adélies on average took the first stint. Male rockhopper penguins may take short turns at brooding the eggs, although the females are more persistent. In a rookery studied by John Warham on Macquarie Island, the egg-laying period was from 8–18 November, and the males started to make for the sea on the 20th, where they spent between nine and seventeen days feeding, leaving the females to incubate the eggs. By 10 December all the females had been relieved by their mates, now fat and sleek, and were back at sea after having been ashore for between thirty-three and forty-five days, incubating for between ten and nineteen days. A similar rota is worked by royal penguins, where the males take turns with the females for the first ten days or so and then depart until the seventeenth day of incubation, when they return to relieve the mate; the females may be back again for the last week's stint.

In little penguins, the extent to which the sexes share the incubation differs from pair to pair; but it was thought that among those studied in Wellington Harbour the females took the chief burden of incubating, and changeovers of duty were made at night. This species is unusual in so far as the incubation period may vary from thirty-three to forty-three days. In many birds the embryos would be killed by any chilling, but live embryos of little penguins were taken from eggs that had not been incubated for at least seven days, following the abandonment of the nests.

It is a widely held fallacy that the emperor and king penguins have pouches in which the eggs are incubated – rather like those which marsupial mammals, such as kangaroos, have for nurturing their young; but they have nothing more than a fold of skin which flops down over their single egg, which is placed against their shanks. The eggs have to be kept warm to allow the embryos to develop, a problem which must be extreme in the sub-zero temperatures

77

Jackass penguins at the entrances to their nesting burrows. In the right foreground there is a young one (*South African Rlys*)

faced by adélie and emperor penguins. Adélies tuck their eggs between the upper sides of the tarsi and the two 'brood patches', so that no part of them comes into contact with the cold ground or air. Whereas the small adélie has to brood lying on its stomach, the taller emperor, with no nest territory, can brood its single egg while standing upright; the bare, vascular brood patches efficiently transfer heat from the adult to the eggs, and the surrounding feathered areas of the skin help to insulate it. When the external temperature was −26°C (−15°F), the internal egg temperature of emperor penguins was 31°C (88°F), some 57°C (103°F) higher than the environment; this speaks well for the effectiveness of the insulation. For the smaller king penguins, the brood-spot temperature was measured at 37·2 to 38·33°C (99 to 101°F) and the eggs were maintained at temperatures varying between 29·45°C and 35·55°C (85°F and 96°F).

The duration of the male's first turn at incubation may, to a large extent, be governed by the distance the female must travel to reach the feeding grounds and replenish her reserves. Emperor females may have to cross many miles of sea ice at the end of June after the eggs are laid, and so the males of this species incubate for the full six weeks it takes for the chicks to hatch. Among the adélies at Signy, the first incubation period by the male is on average eleven days (seven to eighteen), whereas at the Cape Royds rookery where open water is nearer, the figure is about 7·5 days (two to fourteen).

This of course, determines the fasting period which the males must endure from the time they arrive in the rookery during the Antarctic spring, to the time when their mates relieve them at the nest. At Signy it is about forty days, a period only exceeded by that of the male emperor penguins which may be about ninety days, during which time they live off their extensive reserves of fat. In the emperor, the subcutaneous blubber layer is 3–4cm (1–1½in) thick; the bird may, however, lose nearly half its body weight in this period. King penguins lose anything between 0·07–0·23kg (2½–8oz) each day while they are incubating and from the time an adélie penguin arrives at the rookery to the time it is relieved at the nest, one-third of its weight is expended.

The pre-chick stages of most of the penguin species have been discussed in a comparative way, and although there are differences in behaviour between one kind and another, on the whole they conform to a basic pattern. But the emperor penguin demands some attention for itself, because of its aberrant and beautifully adapted breeding behaviour. So as to complete the life cycle within a year, incubation begins at the end of June or early July, in the depths of the Antarctic winter with a head start of four months before the adélie penguins begin their reproduction cycle. As no nests are built, there is

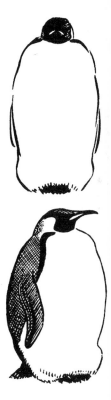

Brooding Emperors

A king penguin incubating its single egg. This is placed in the feet and covered by an abdominal fold of skin. Note the rows of scale-like feathers on the flipper (*Frank W. Lane*)

no bickering and fighting over territories among the males; indeed, should an emperor ever be challenged by another its natural disposition would be to make a dignified retreat.

When compared with those of the closely related king penguin, rookeries of emperor penguins are quiet, with little movement or displaying. However, the apparently lethargic behaviour of incubating male emperors has great survival value for those conditions. After the hens have laid their eggs and started their long trek back to the sea feeding grounds, the males must stand in temperatures regularly ranging down to −40°C (−30°F), perhaps 72°C (130°F) below that of their bodies, with a mean wind velocity of 16–35km (10–22 miles) per hour and occasional blizzards. Nor can they replace energy during this long fast. The eggs must be continuously incubated for six weeks, and should they be exposed for but a few seconds the embryos would be chilled beyond recovery. The emperors' lack of unnecessary movement and strong incubation drive are in fact nice adaptations for conserving energy and for protecting the eggs.

The huddling or clumping behaviour evolved in this species under certain conditions does help to reduce heat loss, and therefore energy, by cutting down the surface area of the body exposed to the cold air. The huddle moves slowly downwind, with the windward birds nudging their way from the flanks into the centre where it is more sheltered from the elements. Such behaviour demands a degree of tolerance that would be unthinkable for the more aggressive species which eschew bodily contact. Apart from their peaceful nature, the emperors' method of incubating their eggs enables them to adopt this way of braving the Antarctic's fiercesome weather. As many as 6,000 may form a cluster – ten to a square metre – should the temperature fall below −10°C (14°F), with strong winds increasing the chill-factor substantially.

There is no doubt as to the effectiveness of huddling as a way of reducing heat loss by between 25 per cent and 50 per cent, thereby economizing on the bird's valuable reserves of fat and oil. Even the emperor's shape, with its comparatively low surface area to volume helps to conserve warmth. These remarkable polar birds even capture 80 per cent of the heat escaping in their breath by an elaborate heat exchange system in their nasal passages. Despite these adaptations, a lone emperor is still insufficiently equipped to cope with the numbing temperatures and shrill winds which are common-place on the Antarctic ice shelf during the winter. To compensate for the heat drain, an isolated bird must raise its body temperature about 2°C (4°F) higher than its huddled companions i.e. 37.9°C (100°F) as opposed to 35.7°C (96°F). Under prolonged harsh conditions an isolated bird would use up its fuel stores sooner and probably die long before those that could get into a huddle.

During their vigil the males shuffle around with the eggs held on their tarsi; movement is so hampered that they must cross even small crevices by falling on to their bills and pushing themselves along with their flippers. Incubating birds take considerable interest in any egg presented to them,

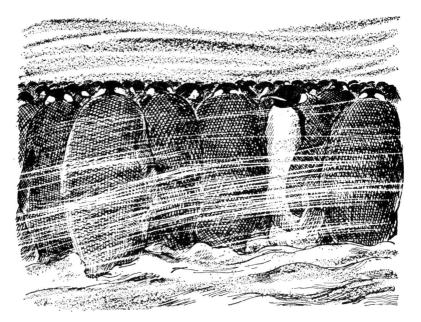

and recently-deprived individuals will take up substitutes, even broken pieces of shell. Significantly, the chief display recorded for emperor penguins is used when a newly-laid egg is transferred from female to male, or in relieving one of the partners of a chick. For this 'Exhibition' display, the emperor first drops the bill on to the chest, then raises the egg fold, giving vent to a very distinctive call; next the head is moved from side to side, showing off its yellow-orange markings. The adélie and gentoo penguins use similar displays during their nest-relief ceremonies. Of all the stereotyped social signals which have been described for other species of penguins, this is the chief one which has been retained by the emperor, which has undergone a drastic economy drive in its movements during the course of evolution.

The breeding season is now well under way; the pairs are formed and the eggs laid, and the parents' lives are geared to the first signs of chipping.

3 · Family Life and Return to the Sea

'That the young of penguins ever see the light of day is somewhat remarkable,' was the comment of one Antarctic traveller who had observed the breeding activities of penguins and organization of the rookeries – which he thought were rife with 'neglect and bad management'. Before seeing how true this statement is, let us first look at what determines the average clutch size in birds, because this will have a direct bearing upon the maximum number of young that a pair can raise.

The ideal number of chicks for a pair of birds is of course the largest number that they are likely to rear successfully. The number of eggs birds lay in each clutch, and therefore the brood size, has just as much survival value to the species as such characteristics as the intricately camouflaged plumage of ground-nesting species or the begging behaviour of nestlings. In those birds in which the young are hatched naked, and are utterly dependent upon the parents for food, warmth and protection, the most frequent clutch size will be that which is likely to produce the largest number of surviving offspring.

The capacity of the parents for bringing in food is obviously limited, so with a larger family each chick will receive less food, and its chances of survival will be accordingly reduced.

But a small family is not necessarily the most efficient, because chicks from small broods need to use more energy to keep warm (large broods can conserve a great deal of heat by huddling), and will therefore need a correspondingly greater amount of food for this purpose alone. Dr T. Royama, of the University of Tokyo, has found while working on great tits that a brood of *three* required as much as about 75 per cent of the total food required by a brood of *eight*; so the brood size which most efficiently converts the food brought by the parents into a further generation of great tits is around eight. However, this figure will vary from one species to another and within the same species will be adjusted to the local food supply. Thick-billed nutcrackers (jay-like birds of the northern coniferous forests) feed their young on hazelnuts gathered and stored during the previous autumn. In seasons following a good crop of hazelnuts, when their caches were large, the birds tended to lay four eggs, but only three if nuts had been scarce, and the winter store was poor. Birds of prey such as short-eared and snowy owls may lay many more eggs in years when there are plagues of voles and lemmings respectively.

Sea birds, like shearwaters, auks, and penguins, only lay small clutches, with on average two eggs at most; albatrosses, and both emperor and king penguins, only produce one egg each season. Many sea birds are comparatively long-lived, and the theory was put forward that the fertility of these species had been reduced, so that the recruitment of young birds into the population should nicely balance the low mortality of the adults. However, there is now accumulating evidence that one or two young are as many as the parents can feed. For example, should one of a pair of yellow-eyed penguins die while rearing two vigorously-growing chicks, the surviving parent can bring in only enough food for one chick; and the stronger one will soon monopolize that, continuing to grow normally while the other grows weaker

Yellow-eyed penguin (*John Warham*)

and starves to death. As one parent alone has not the food-bringing capacity to rear two chicks, it is obvious that in this and probably other species of penguins no pair could raise four chicks, and perhaps not even three. The normal clutch of two may well be the most efficient brood size for the smaller penguin species. However, the average clutch size may vary with the age of the hen. For instance, young and inexperienced adélies may lay only one egg per season, but by the time they are six years old, they may tend to produce clutches of two. Even so, mortality can be very high, with adélies raising only 62 per cent of their chicks to the crèche stage, and kings rearing only 25 per cent of their offspring in some localities.

Other information about the survival value of 'normal' family sizes has been obtained by scientists who have artificially increased the number of young in certain nests, and compared the growth and mortality rates with those of normal-sized broods. These kinds of experiments have not yet been carried out on penguins, but in shearwaters the results have been revealing. Shearwaters are long-lived oceanic birds, and the single chick is tended by the parents in a burrow nest, and develops over a period of six or seven weeks. As it hatches, the experimenter adds another chick which has recently emerged from an egg. The parents cannot supply enough nourishment for two hungry youngsters, with the result that both become emaciated and more often than not one dies; among Manx shearwaters on the Island of Skomer, for every five pairs artificially supplied with twins, only two chicks were reared (an average of 0.4 young reared per pair), whereas nearly every pair with a normal brood managed to rear their single chick (an average of 0·95 young reared per pair).

The results of these twinning experiments show that any deviation from the normal clutch size produces fewer young. However, every egg does not necessarily produce a chick, as among those penguin species which occasionally lay three eggs the third and smallest one is usually infertile, or

at least rarely hatches, an odd and wasteful practice. White-flippered penguins generally lay two eggs, but in some years no less than 57 per cent of them fail to hatch for reasons that are not yet clear.

By and large, though, the effectiveness of the pairs in hatching their clutches may depend upon their previous experience as parents; this means that birds breeding for the first time may be less competent than older birds, a generalization which is borne out by careful scientific observations. In his renowned study of the yellow-eyed penguin, which was spread over eighteen years, L. E. Richdale found that of eighty-six two-year-old females which bred, 62 per cent laid two eggs and 32 per cent hatched at least one; the overall success of this group in rearing young was 18 per cent, a very low figure when compared with that for older penguins. However, the hatching success improved markedly with the increasing age of the female parent and stood at 78 per cent for three-year-old birds and 95 per cent for fully-matured females four years of age and over.

Inefficient incubation behaviour is not the basic cause of the comparative failure of young birds to fledge their young. Fertility itself varies with age; older birds tend to be more likely to produce fertile eggs, whatever their previous experience of breeding. Investigation shows that in two-year-old yellow-eyed penguins, only 32 per cent of the fully incubated eggs hatch, and in three-year-old individuals which laid for the first time, the corresponding figure was 70 per cent; thereafter in four-year-old birds 92 per cent of the fully-incubated eggs could be expected to hatch, showing a threefold jump in fertility in two or three years. It seems that the physiological machinery of female yellow-eyed penguins is not developed to the full until they reach the age of four years.

If the two-year-olds among yellow-eyed penguins are so relatively infecund, why do they attempt to breed at all? The first one or two years in the rookery can be looked upon as an apprentice period, because although as a group they may be able to add only a few individuals to the next generation, they do acquire valuable experience by joining in the general foray of the rookeries, learning how to hold their territories and how to incubate; this will pay dividends during the forth-coming years, when the females at least have reached their maximum fertility.

Taking a further example from another well-studied species, only 2,500 out of an estimated 3,600 adélie penguins at Cape Royds were recorded as nesting successfully; therefore the potential number of breeding pairs was in fact 33 per cent above the actual number of breeders. A possible explanation is that latecomers to the rookery tend not to breed, because they are inexperienced and because they miss the aphrodisiac effect of the breeding displays, which have passed their peak before they arrive. As with the yellow-eyed penguins, experienced adélies breed more successfully than beginners, their failure rate in egg-laying and chick-rearing being only one-third of the overall failure rate for the rookery. Even birds in their first year may hang around the rookeries, and in adélies and the crested species these can be distinguished from adults by their white, not black, chins.

Penguin chicks may take up to three days to chip their way out of the eggs, and when they first emerge they are covered with fluffy or woolly down, although again the emperor penguins differ, their young being almost naked; they would freeze to death in a few minutes if left unattended, and the presence of insulating fluff would merely hinder the passage of heat from the parent's brood spot to the chick. At first, the young penguins are far from endearing; each resembles a pear-shaped sac for accommodating and digesting food, supported on a pair of ungainly, big feet and surmounted by a puny head. Although cosseted by its parents, the chick's prospects may depend upon who is incubating at the time of hatching. In the case of rockhoppers, there is heavy mortality at this crucial time. Chicks stand the best chance of surviving if their mother has already returned from the sea laden with the benison of the ocean for her newly emerged brood. The males who may have taken the last major stint of incubation are usually unable to offer the hatchlings anything except a

Adult and young macaroni penguins (*Niall Rankin*)

few drops of unappetizing mucus. This is the time when each cock needs the support of his mate, who can stagger back from the sea with 20–30 per cent of her weight of krill, fish and squid, to feed the chicks who would otherwise go hungry. Nevertheless, only two out of five chicks (40 per cent) survive, at least on the Falkland Islands. From the moment of hatching the chicks are tenaciously brooded, until they are too large to be effectively placed between the brood spot and tarsi; and of course this corresponds to the age when they are able to maintain their own body heat.

There must be some degree of co-operation between the parents in order to rear their young successfully. Predators are an ever-present menace, and a few minutes of lowered vigilance on the part of the adults guarding a nest may invite a pursuing skua to make off with the chick and therefore waste the weeks of courtship and incubation. While the chick or chicks are young, they are particularly vulnerable; while one parent goes off to collect food for the almost insatiable youngsters, the other must stand on guard over the nest. Even in the burrow-nesting little penguins, the chicks are not left alone for the first ten or twenty days of their lives. In the Antarctic pygoscelids the guard stage lasts about a month, when one or other of the parents stands on duty after returning from the sea with a crop full of food. Duties such as feeding and guarding are carried out equally by both sexes, excepting in the crested species where it is the male who stands guard continuously while the female takes over the job of bringing food to the chick. The duration of the guard period varies; in the royal penguin it may last from two to three weeks, and in the smaller rockhopper it may be thirty days, after which the chicks' need for food has become more than one parent can satiate. In any case, it means that the male has to endure a fast of up to forty days. Among those penguins in which there is a division of labour between the sexes the females take the first incubation shift, and this is presumably to allow the males to return to the sea to fatten up and prepare themselves for a four- or five-week fast while guarding the chicks in the first few weeks of life. It would be interesting to find out why the crested species have not evolved a system of sharing all duties. After the 'guard' stage, the chicks of surface-nesting species adopt other forms of behaviour that help to prevent their falling prey to skuas and gulls.

The race to satisfy the chicks' insatiable hunger, which increases with their rapid growth, presents no problems to species nesting close to the sea; but emperor penguins, at their rookeries on the fast sea ice miles away from open water, must properly organize the first feeding shifts between the parents. The chick generally hatches beneath its father who has cosseted the egg alone for about sixty days. Should his mate be delayed then he feeds his tiny and vulnerable offspring for a few days not upon the contents of his crop, for surely he has none left, but upon a remarkable oesophageal secretion comprising 60 per cent protein and 28 per cent fat. However this offering of 'penguin's milk' is meant to be only a stop-gap measure to tide the tiny creature over until its mother turns up with her crop full of nourishing goodies. The females relieve the now emaciated males, who in turn trail off to the sea to feed, to build up their depleted reserves and to collect food for their chicks. It was thought that the returning females solicited chicks at random from the possessive males; but each female apparently recognizes its own mate, and with appropriate ceremonies takes over the correct offspring. As each parent carries about 3kg (7lb) of fish and squid in its crop, it can carry on regularly regurgitating food for the small chick for some while, until the other mate returns with fresh supplies of fish, crustacea or squid, the nourishing harvest of the nearby seas.

The irresistible brooding drive and its importance to the emperors has already been mentioned. It will often extend also, for a short time, to any chick temporarily abandoned by its parent. A chickless adult, or even an older chick, will brood it long enough to save it from freezing until the parent returns. The chief characteristic which arouses interest in an abandoned youngster is movement; little notice is taken of dead ones.

Emperor feeding young

92

Young penguins are quite different from the adults in their colouration and patterning. The down is usually uniformly greyish, but young adélies may be any colour from silvery grey to charcoal black – a peculiar kind of variation – with the head darker than the rest of the body: these differences disappear when they reach ten days, beause they then moult into a charcoal-black, woolly down. By far the most striking are the young emperors; once they have left their parents' brood spots, their bodies are covered with grey down, lighter on the back, and their white cheeks contrast with a black area extending over the top of the head and neck. As they stand around the rookery they look like pilots of the early days of aircraft, wearing helmets equipped with ear muffs.

Probably these conspicuous colour patterns help to make

Emperor penguins and chicks. The left-hand chick is emerging from between the abdominal fold of skin and feet of the parent. The adult on the left-hand side is asleep, and has its bill tucked behind the flipper (*Jean Prévost*)

the chicks stand out against the surrounding snow and ice, and this would be valuable to emperor penguins, which have no individual nest site where the young can be found. In all species the special colouration gives the young a certain degree of immunity from the bickering and fighting so often rampant in the rookeries. As they wander around, they are recognized as presenting no kind of threat to breeding adults, and are not considered as competitors for mates or nesting sites; their appearance may help to inhibit any kind of rage or fear in the adults, eliciting parental behaviour from them instead. Although the need for crypticity or camouflage determines the colouring of many juvenile birds, penguins and indeed colonial sea birds nesting on protected sites dispense with it; they rely upon the presence of a large number of adults or older youngsters to intimidate their enemies.

Every species has its characteristic growth rate. The little penguins desert their offspring when they are about fifty days old and have reached their maximum weight, and this species has the shortest breeding cycle of all. Five months after hatching, in the Antarctic autumn, emperor penguins are only three-quarters grown, and the king penguin has a breeding cycle of fifteen months, the longest of any bird; this, together with its survival value, will be described later.

Penguins spend some time grooming their young – not necessarily a sign of affection. One writer has suggested that king penguins do this when their crops are empty as a means of reducing the chicks' call for food. There is certainly evidence in other birds that parents may be tempted to attack over-persistent young; the initially aggressive response often changes to preening. Parents entering crèches, the big groups of young ones, seem to get rough treatment as the chicks attempt to induce regurgitation, and the fact that the young are rarely attacked testifies to the efficiency of the chicks in appeasing adults. They nevertheless fail occasionally; adélie rookeries may harbour rogue adults liable to kill immature individuals. There is also one well-authenticated case of a parent adélie which was involved in a fight with one of its

Gentoo Penguin
family.

94

Gentoo penguin with its two chicks (*John Warham*)

neighbours; it lost the encounter, then returned to its own nest and battered its chick to death in a fit of rage. This 'redirected' response is well known among other animals, including humans, among whom it is sometimes labelled as 'whipping the office boy'.

As the young penguins grow and become mobile, they assemble into small groups; the yellow-eyed species collect on the pathways leading to the sea. These aggregations of young birds still dependent on their parents are a well-developed feature of rookery life of some penguin species, and are known as crèches; however the term crèche does not cover the chance gathering of juveniles to be found in any socially-breeding birds such as gannets or gulls. Breeding emperor, king, adélie, chinstrap, gentoo and rockhopper penguins – in fact all those living in the more southerly latitudes – form these nurseries, but none of the burrow-nesting *Spheniscus* or *Eudyptula* species do so; nor do the more temperate or subtropical 'crested' penguins (*Eudyptes* species).

The ages when the chicks start to gather vary from species to species, and probably from rookery to rookery, according to the rate at which they can grow. Adélie penguins at the Cape Royds rookery enter crèches on about their twenty-second day, but in the more rigorous conditions at Signy they may be about thirty days old. Rockhoppers tend to form crèches at sixteen days of age, whereas chicks of the larger species, kings and emperors, may be guarded by their parents until they reach thirty-five or forty days; after this, both parents can leave to seek food. The proximity of large numbers of other youngsters may be a great incentive to crèche-forming; adélie chicks on the periphery of the rookeries tend to group less readily than those from nests in the centre, a fact which may have a bearing upon their reduced chances of survival. The chicks remain in these bunches for some time, although rockhoppers may return to their nest sites to be fed. As they grow larger they tend to disperse, spending more and more time at the nest site; adélie penguins start to do this when about fifty-six days old. The

Crèche of young Adélie
Penguins. A Skua has
killed a chick which
had wandered away
from the crèche.

Nursery group of Eider
ducklings which are able
to feed independently
from hatching.

Crèches are formed by
young Greater Flamingoes
awaiting the return of
their parents with food.

number of crèches declines as the chicks grow older, because the smaller groups tend to coalesce.

Communal nursery systems are rare in birds, being found only in the flamingoes and in the eider and king-eider ducks; the ducklings, after being led to sea by the parents for feeding, tend to gather into rafts, accompanied by a few older juveniles; but the ducklings do not rely upon the parents for food as, unlike young flamingoes and penguins, they can dabble for planktonic organisms as soon as they reach the water.

The nursery groups found in baboons prove useful for promoting play activities: young monkeys have a strong exploratory urge and play with anything that responds in a satisfying way; other young monkeys play better than anything else! But young penguins do not play; so the reason for the temporary banding into crèches has been much discussed.

Adélie Penguin with identifying flipper-ring.

It was formerly thought that the crèche was a kind of communal infant-rearing system which allowed the strongest chicks to be fed by incoming adults, in conditions where two birds could not collect enough food to rear their own chicks. This ingenious suggestion was neatly demolished when ringing experiments proved that parents only disgorge their crop contents to their own chicks – recognized, presumably, by their calls as well as their appearance. Dr W. J. Sladen marked a number of adult adélies and their young. Only once did he find an adult feeding a strange chick, and even then it passed but a small amount of food. If the parents disappeared, their chicks within the crèche starved to death, even though surrounded by adults disgorging food to their own persistently begging young. Each crèche contains chicks of varying ages, and the fact that the youngest are maintained in good health shows that they do not have to compete with the more boisterous older ones for food, confirming that each chick is fed by its own parents. King penguins have also been investigated and are known to feed none but their own chicks, though they sometimes will go through the motions of feeding when accosted by others.

A crèche of emperor penguin chicks (*Jean Prévost, Expeditions Polaires Françaises*)

The theory that the crèches of young birds are protected by adults cannot be substantiated; unoccupied adults sometimes hang around the crèches, but they are not organized into any sort of guard system. Nevertheless, if faced with danger, chicks at the crèche age may concentrate around an adult bird, not necessarily a parent, and this behaviour may in itself afford them a degree of immunity from skua attacks.

Nor is inherent gregariousness an adequate explanation for the chicks' behaviour. As most of the Antarctic species form crèches, and for some of the time the chicks huddle together, much as emperor adults will do during bitter weather, it has been thought that heat conservation might be their purpose. It cannot be denied that they will be able to conserve some heat, this explanation does not seem to be the overridingly important one, except possibly among emperors. Crèche formation does not in any case coincide with particularly adverse spells of weather.

After long and patient watching and recording of the response of these aggregations of young birds to different conditions in the rookery, biologists have concluded that the crèche is, for penguins and probably also for flamingoes and eider ducks, an anti-predator device, working on the prin-

99

ciple of safety in numbers. As the chicks grow larger and their appetites increase correspondingly, the energies of *both* parents must be turned toward bringing in a continuous supply of food. At the crèche-forming stage the chicks are at a vulnerable part of their life-cycle – unattended, and though active enough to keep warm, not capable of warding off the attacks of birds to which they would fall easy prey. Antarctic skuas, giant petrels and various kinds of gulls ever patrol the rookeries of the species which form crèches. None of these birds is any match for an adult penguin, which can battle powerfully with both flippers, but an unattended chick, perhaps half the size of its parents, can easily be out-manoeuvred and eviscerated. Skuas will not, however, enter a crèche – although there is little evidence to suppose that the chicks would retaliate should one do so. If a predacious bird approaches, the crèche becomes consolidated, the chicks bunching together, and those nearby of similar age quickly seek safety in the cluster, which then moves away *en masse*. The marauder loses interest as soon as a pursued chick reaches the group.

Rowland Taylor has shown the effectiveness of the crèche in reducing chick mortality through skua attacks on adélies at Cape Royds. Out of thirty-seven ringed chicks kept under daily observation and which eventually died, twenty-two (i.e. nearly three-quarters) of the twenty-eight lost during the guard stage fell to the skuas; but of the further nine lost during the crèche stage, only three (one-third) were accounted for by skuas. Desertion by the parents and exposure were the next most frequent causes of chick mortality.

Why some of the other surface-nesting crested species have not evolved crèche behaviour is a mystery. Possibly the adults can more effectively deal with avian predators and thus protect their young, or else the predation pressure may be less severe at the stage when both parents must be employed in collecting food. The young of burrow-nesters, or those using some cover during the nesting season, are naturally protected more effectively than open nesters.

Most of the smaller kinds of penguins which nest in the

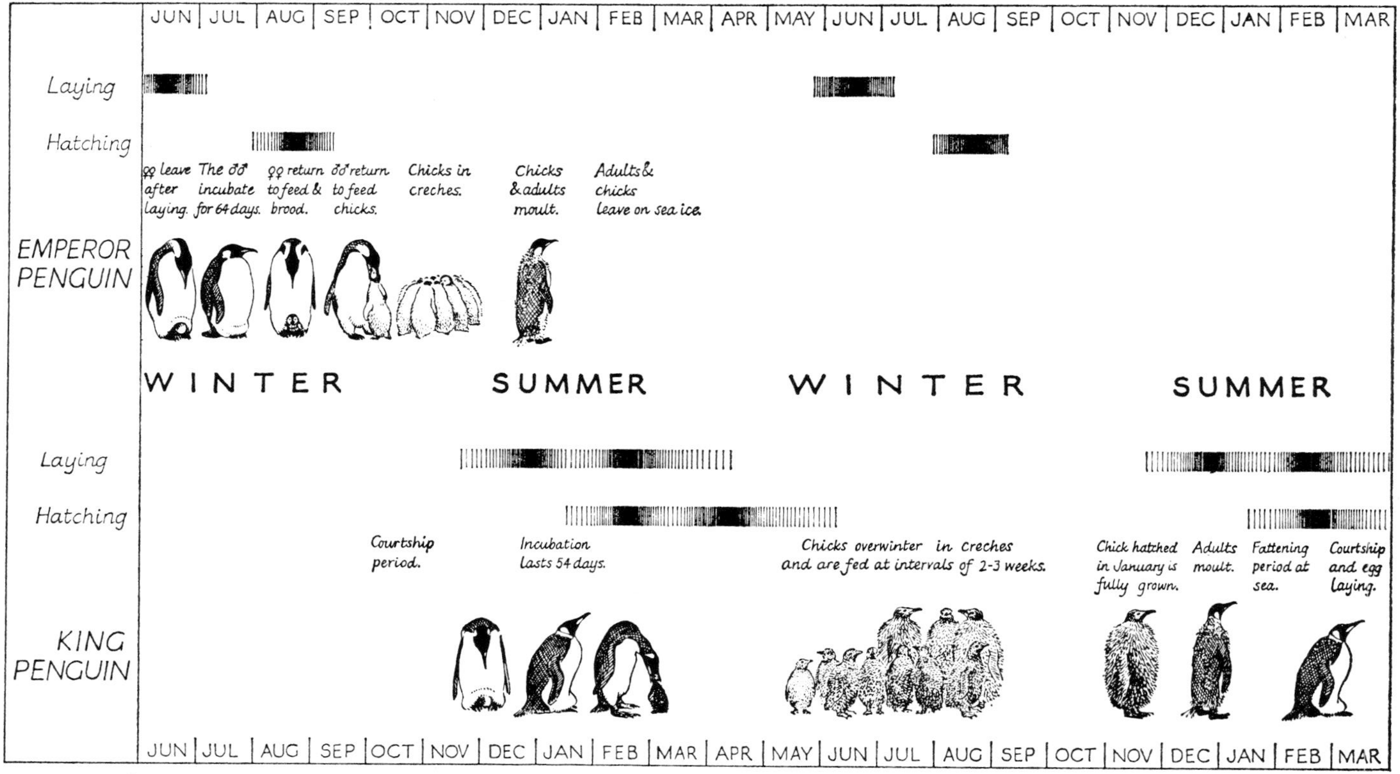
JUN JUL AUG SEP OCT NOV DEC JAN FEB MAR APR MAY JUN JUL AUG SEP OCT NOV DEC JAN FEB MAR
Laying
Hatching
♀♀ leave after laying.
The ♂♂ incubate for 64 days.
♀♀ return to feed & brood.
♂♂ return to feed chicks.
Chicks in creches.
Chicks & adults moult.
Adults & chicks leave on sea ice.
EMPEROR PENGUIN
WINTER
SUMMER
WINTER
SUMMER
Laying
Hatching
Courtship period.
Incubation lasts 54 days.
Chicks overwinter in creches and are fed at intervals of 2-3 weeks.
Chick hatched in January is fully grown.
Adults moult.
Fattening period at sea.
Courtship and egg laying.
KING PENGUIN
JUN JUL AUG SEP OCT NOV DEC JAN FEB MAR APR MAY JUN JUL AUG SEP OCT NOV DEC JAN FEB MAR

Diagram to show the differences in the breeding cycles between the closely related Emperor and King Penguins. The Emperors take advantage of the short chick rearing period in the low Antarctic by incubating their eggs through the winter so that they are ready to start feeding at the first opportunity in the Spring. The more sub-antarctic King Penguins begin to breed later in the Spring. There are two peaks in egg laying. Adults laying in November are ready to start breeding again during the second egg laying period of the following season, taking anything up to fifteen months to complete the cycle. Emperors can breed every year wheras Kings can only do so twice in every three breeding seasons.

deep south are able to do so because they squeeze their reproductive activities into the relatively brief Antarctic spring and summer when food is plentiful. The two larger species, the king and emperor, have a more formidable task and are unable to compress their nesting schedule sufficiently. They have therefore adopted quite different strategies for coping with the high southern latitudes. The kings are spurred into courtship during the sub-Antarctic spring, like several of the smaller Pygoscelids. But their chicks fail to grow and moult in time to fledge before the winter blizzards set in. They therefore postpone the moment of becoming independent of their parents, surviving the winter in crèches on starvation rations, and fledging the following spring, 14–16 months after hatching. The mighty emperor overcomes the difficulty imposed by the short summer, by bringing forward the egg laying period into the winter. In this way no time is lost when the sun peeps above the horizon, stimulating a flush of marine productivity. The price that the emperor pays is that the youngsters fledge to face their first winter barely 60 per cent of their adult weight. Mortality is therefore often high, particularly when 40 per cent of the seasons eggs and offspring may perish. Nevertheless by cramming their breeding into a single season, the adult emperors can at least nest every year.

The length of the king penguin's breeding cycle is only rivalled by that of the Californian condor and the royal albatross: both of these take one year to rear their young, but the adults probably breed only in alternate years, taking a year to recuperate. The king penguin does rather better, breeding twice every three years, and it is because of this that its egg-laying period is drawn out over several months. Those birds which lay during late November of one breeding season can sometimes start breeding again by the February of the next one, fifteen months later, after their young have dispersed. Eggs laid after February have little chance of hatching – if they do, then the young will probably not survive the onset of winter in May, because in that short time they will not have accumulated enough fat: spending the

Snares island penguin. Adults and chicks ready for leaving the rookery
(*John Warham*)

winter in the crèche, with only one feeding session every two to three weeks, king penguin chicks have to draw heavily on their reserves.

A fat start to life is literally crucial to a young king. In the summer, with adults bringing them as much as 1kg (say 2lb) of fish or squid each hour, the young put on weight fast and by the onset of winter they may weight about 11–13kg (24–28lb), much of it in the form of subcutaneous fat two or more centimetres (¾in) thick in places. During the frigid winter, they will need this fuel to sustain life. Huddled in their crèches between May and June, each chick burns up its subcutaneous fat at the rate of 0·06kg (2oz) each day, depending upon the severity of the weather and how much food the parents deliver. Of course, it is not really necessary to roman-

Fully feathered white flippered penguin chicks in their nest (sub-species of little penguin) (*John Warham*)

ticize this feat of endurance which by human standards would be remarkable indeed; to the penguins it is inevitable, and they are well constructed to undertake it. With the arrival of spring begins the race to tip the scales at 19–21kg (42–46lb) before they face their second winter and their first moult, an equally energy-consuming business.

By comparison, the more northerly *Spheniscus* species have an easier time – or did until historical times. Being mostly inshore feeders and not having to cope with vast ice fields, they have no breeding fast. The members of each pair tend to relieve each other daily. Two chicks are often reared, one leaving the burrow as much as a month or more before its smaller sibling, which often catches up, even exceeding the weight of the more advanced brother or sister. Unfortunately, the commercial removal of the guano 'cap' from islands into which jackass and humboldt penguins used to burrow has forced many of these birds to nest on the surface.

Nowadays, predatory gulls can make inroads into the crop of both eggs and young chicks to an extent hitherto impossible.

While the chicks are in the crèches, the furry down is soon replaced by feathers. When adélie penguins are twenty to twenty-five days old, the down is lost from beneath the flippers and ten days later the quills are poking through in various parts of the body. At forty-five days of age the immature plumage is obvious and five days later the last fluff has left the fully formed feathers. The young penguin is then ready to face the life at sea to which its 60–100 million years of continuous evolution has adapted it. It will not, however, plunge into the sea straight away when its time comes to leave the land; adélies certainly visit the water at least once before final departure for the pack ice.

It is after the birds have left the rough-and-tumble of

Penguin chicks

Adélie

Little

Emperor

Rockhopper

Gentoo

rookery life that they may be seen to play. One of the most enchanting games described for the smaller Antarctic species is popular on parts of the coast where ice floes are moving close into the shore. Adélie penguins line the shore waiting for a suitable slab of ice to pass, jump onto it and apparently revel in being taken for a ride. Further down the coast they leave their floe and make their way back to the starting point to wait for another.

At the end of the breeding season, the adults, too, lose their old plumage. In chinstrap and yellow-eyed penguins, non-breeding birds moult first, followed by unsuccessful breeders, and finally by those that have been busy rearing chicks. Feathers do not last indefinitely; they become frayed through their constant rubbing against each other and through contact with the ground and water; no doubt even the owner's regular preening helps wear them out. Then there are the parasites which grow fat on the substance, keratin, of which feathers are made, not to mention the occasional losses in the course of quarrels with mate or competitor. So once a year the plumage is moulted; this must be done on *terra firma*, often on the nest site, because a penguin must have watertight plumage before it can swim. Although a small proportion of adélies moult on land, by and large they do so in the pack ice, remaining for two weeks on top of the ice floes without venturing into the water. Should water flood through gaps in the feathers to the air spaces and the skin, the birds would chill and the plumage would be waterlogged, a situation that quickly leads to shock, pneumonia and death.

Moulting Little Penguin

A little penguin moulting. There is a large tick embedded in the head between the bill and eye (*John Warham*)

When the chicks have left the nest, little penguins start a period of intensive feeding to reach the physical condition necessary to enable them to withstand a moulting session. On coming ashore prior to moulting, they are heavier than normal, and their feathers, far from being greyish-blue, are tinged with brown after the year's wear and tear. Dr F. Kinsky relates of the little penguins of the Wellington Harbour area:

At this stage, the bird enters a burrow or other place of shelter and settles down for the actual moult. During the first two to three days, there appears to be no visible change, except that the swelling of the skin tissues, which had already started before settling down, increases. This swelling is specially noticeable on the flippers, which now readily bleed when knocked. From the fourth day onwards the old feathers no longer lie flat, due to the pressure of the new feathers growing underneath. At this stage, the bird appears to be still larger than normal, but its weight is already falling considerably. On the fifth or sixth day, the old

107

feathers adhering to the tips of the new growing feathers start falling off, and the first to go are those on the flippers, face, and lower back. The last old feathers to go are on the forehead, middle back, and on the flipper bases. Usually on the thirteenth to fifteenth day, all old feathers have been shed, and the bird spends much time preening and shaking the sheaths out of its new feathers. Within two days, the swelling of the skin tissues recedes and the bird leaves at any time during the night and returns to water.

Yellow-eyed and white-flippered penguins apparently moult in their nest burrows, but on Somes Island only about 20 per cent of the adults may be found crouched in their nesting sites. During moulting the birds tend to be rather

A freshly moulted erect-crested penguin (*John Warham*)

quiet and less quarrelsome, conserving their energy, and this may also have survival value. Emperor penguins have to moult on the pack ice after leaving their young at the end of the Antarctic summer. Groups of these birds may be seen at this time looking ragged and pathetic, marooned on their ice floes, stained with several weeks' worth of bile-coloured excrement. Before the moult, penguins feed avidly, and put on a great deal of weight in the form of fat. Adult king penguins usually weigh 13–14kg (28–30lb), but just before their prenuptial moult they weigh about 19–21kg (42–46lb) and look like animated barrels of fat. At the end of their moult they weigh about 14kg (30lb) and have used up about 0·2kg (7oz) per day. Yellow-eyed penguins lose up to 45 per cent of their body weight during the four weeks it takes them to renew their plumage. No less remarkable are the figures for white-flippered penguins, which turn the scales at about 1·6kg (3lb 10oz) just before their moulting season, and at the end of it are a mere 0·9kg (2lb) – a drop of nearly one-half of their body weight, during a period when their bodily activity is working literally at fever pitch to produce a new plumage. This is illustrated by an increase in their body temperature from 38·6°C (101·6°F) to 39·5°C (103·1°F) during the moult.

Thus ends the penguin's year. From the egg hatches an awkward, fluffy creature which by the time it reaches the sea will already have bypassed many dangers, some by chance, others by its own skill. To finish the quotation which opened this chapter: 'If a young bird is tenacious enough to reach the adult stages, it deserves to live.' And so they do!

Moulting King Penguin

Moulting Jackass Penguin

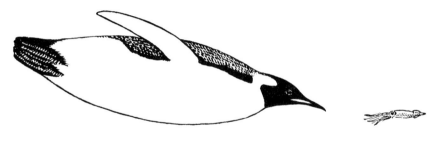

4 · Food and Predators

Penguins are marine hunters and share the southern oceans with a host of other sea creatures with whom they vie to make a living. In the Antarctic alone, six kinds of penguins comprise 90 per cent of the bird biomass, and may consume no less than 50 per cent, and perhaps as much as 70 per cent of the sea's resources. At the peak of the breeding season, 5 million adélies nesting on Lawrie Island catch a stupendous 9,000 tonnes (8,800 tons) of krill and small fish *daily*, and that is equivalent to the capacity of seventy modern trawlers!

No less than 70 per cent of so called planet Earth is in fact ocean, and a mere 15 per cent of this accounts for the relative shallows of the continental and island shelves where most penguins go about their business. The sixteen (or eighteen!) kinds belong to a select club of pelagic birds. Of 9,016 or so avian species now recognized, only about 300 are truly marine, that is, outside of the nesting season, spend their lives entirely away from the coast. Far more terrestial species have evolved for two reasons. A large number of ecological niches are available on the land, and diversity is encouraged as evolution proceeds independently on separate land masses, and on either sides of mountain barriers. The number of species that evolve therefore tend to be greater than the number of niches; for example, in Australia, there are no woodpeckers, their 'place' is taken by certain kinds of cockatoos which have specialized in extracting insects from tree trunks. But all the oceans are confluent, and as sea birds

Royal penguins. The female is feeding the chick (*John Warham*)

are prodigious travellers this tends to lend an overall uniformity to their populations; there are few barriers in the oceans to separate populations of birds as there are on land, although the equatorial doldrums may have prevented wind-loving albatrosses from successfully reinvading the Northern Atlantic after the last Ice Age.

But what the pelagic birds lack in variety they make up in numbers. Charles Darwin commented wrongly as it now seems, that the most numerous avian species was undoubtedly a sea bird; he picked out the fulmar, but James Fisher, some hundred years later – leaving aside the domestic chicken – awarded the distinction to another Arctic seabird, the little auk or dovekie. Others have put their money on Wilson's petrel, the flocks of which darken the sky over their breeding grounds on sub-Antarctic islands; although difficult to estimate, there may be 100 million. The sooty tern, a graceful black and white inhabitant of reefs and sub-tropical islands with pelagic feeding habits also ranks as one of the most numerous of birds. By comparison penguins are rare! Perhaps the adélie is the most common, with the largest rookeries totalling half a million pairs. Five million couples of macaroni penguins breed on South Georgia; one world estimate for rockhoppers was 4¾ million pairs, and 2 million royals nest at Maquarie Island. Such is the fecundity of certain areas of the ocean that on the islands off the coast of Peru, 100,000 tons of guano may be deposited each year by millions of sea birds, chiefly guanay cormorants, boobies and brown pelicans, which feed in that cool, misty area of the Pacific. About 2½ million giant shearwaters breed in burrows principally on Nightingale, one of the islands of Tristan da Cunha. The northern hemisphere is no less prolific than the south in its sea birds: the loomeries of Scoresby Sound and the Liverpool coast of East Greenland contain perhaps five million little auks or dovekies. The crowded bird cliffs and island buttresses which girdle the temperate and sub-Arctic regions of the globe bear witness to the astonishing numbers of sea birds, and also to the fecundity of the seas which support them.

These colossal populations are not, however, distributed evenly over the seas, and their adjacent coasts. The impressive bird cliffs of the north to which the auks return to breed, and indeed the penguin rookeries in the southern hemisphere, are not located at random within the area theoretically available to them. The eminently suitable cliffs in the Aegean Sea do not ring to the chatter of guillemots or dovekies, any more than rookeries of penguins thrive on any equatorial islands; apart from a few on the Galapagos group. The key to their siting is, of course, the availability of food.

The complex forces which govern the productivity of the seas ultimately determine the distribution of penguins and indeed of all sea birds.

Plants, whether grasses, trees or seaweeds, are the world's *primary producers* of food. By the process of photosynthesis

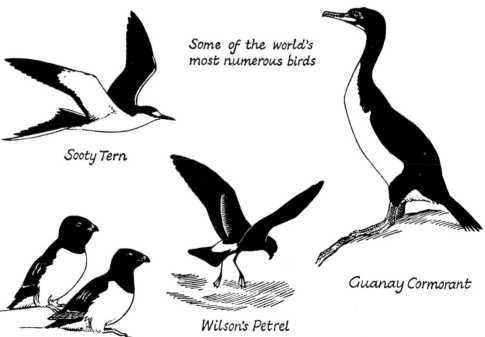

Some of the world's most numerous birds

Sooty Tern

Guanay Cormorant

Little Auk

Wilson's Petrel

they absorb and harness some of the radiant energy of the sun and lock this up in the form of carbohydrates (sugars), proteins, oils or fats which they manufacture. These energy-rich compounds stored by plants are then available to animals. In the web of life, it is the role of grazing animals, such as deer, rabbits or water-fleas, not only to use some of this energy, but also to convert and store some of it in a different form, which is then in turn cropped by carnivorous species, like foxes and pike. When the carnivores die, their bodies will be broken down by bacteria and fungi, releasing ample nutriments into the soil or sea which ultimately will be taken up again by the primary producers.

In the sea, the primary producers are the microscopic plants of the plankton – the diatoms. It has been estimated that the sea's photosynthetic capability would allow the annual production of 33 million tons of food, of which only 0·3 per cent is at present harvested by man. Put another way, under favourable conditions, each square metre of sea can 'fix' 20g (0·8oz per square yard) of carbon daily. The tiny floating plants that constitute the phyto-plankton are then the starting points of the food chains which lead to penguins and to all pelagic birds, seals, whales, porpoises and so on. By and large the more planktonic plants that an area of sea can support, the more of the larger carnivores like birds that can live there.

Phyto-plankton production is, however, limited by various factors. Light is a very important one; as the diatoms need radiant energy from the sun to carry out their process of photosynthesis, the fertility of the sea will be reduced where the level of illumination is low, as it is in Antarctica and the Arctic in their respective winters. The presence of fertilizing minerals, like phosphates and nitrates is as essential for plant production in the sea as it is in the kitchen garden, and so any scarcity of them will inhibit phyto-plankton growth; the minerals can only be replenished by the decomposition of dead planktonic organisms or by animal excrement. As dead, pelagic organisms sink, so valuable nutrients tend to be lost from the photosynthetic layers of the sea to the deeper, colder layers, where they accumulate. This is why some tropical waters are not able to support as much life as the favourable light conditions might lead one to expect; the surface layers are relatively depleted of nutrient minerals. But the oceans are by no means static, and the constant circulation brings enough of the deeper mineral-rich layers to the surface to produce flushes of plankton, thus increasing the number of those animals which feed on it.

The water near the Equator receives much more heat than that at the poles, and so convection currents tend to stir the oceans. But forces exerted by the rotation of the earth (Coriolis Force) impart a rotary movement to these currents, and set in motion an anticlockwise swirl in the South Atlantic, Pacific and Indian Oceans. Similar convection

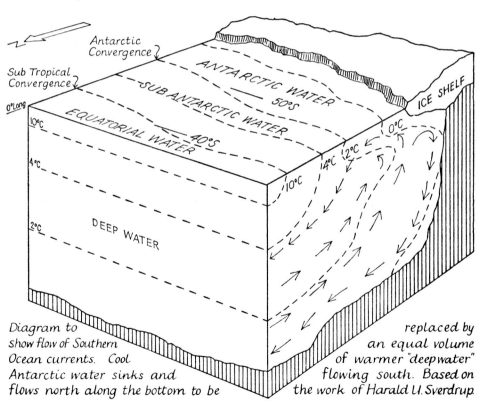

Diagram to show flow of Southern Ocean currents. Cool Antarctic water sinks and flows north along the bottom to be replaced by an equal volume of warmer "deepwater" flowing south. Based on the work of Harald U. Sverdrup.

currents within the atmosphere produce the well-known trade winds which, in the southern hemisphere, blow westwards off the continents of South Africa and South America. These affect the distribution of penguins because by the constant pressure they exert on the sea off the west coast of those continents, the surface waters are blown away and are replaced by nutrient-rich water welling up from deeper layers (about 300m/327yd) off the edge of the continental shelf. The cool Benguelan current thus supports large populations of sea birds and many hundreds of thousands of jackass penguins off the otherwise tropical African coast.

Similarly the more powerful Humboldt current moves implacably up the west coast of South America for thousands of miles at a speed of about 3·7km per hour (2 knots). Near to the Equator it is deflected towards the Galapagos Islands where it merges into the South Equatorial drift. The temperature of the sea only varies from about 14·4 to 17·8°C (57·9 to 64°F) over its range from the tip of South America to the point at which it is deflected westwards, and this proves that it consists mostly of cool water brought to the surface by off-shore winds. The fertility of this strip of water, only a few miles wide and hunted by magellanic, peruvian, galapagos, rockhopper and macaroni penguins, is reflected in the guano production of Peru, together with the vast anchovy harvest used to be reaped off that coast. The galapagos penguin is able to inhabit the equatorial Galapagos Islands solely by virtue of their being washed by the Humboldt current; their climate is made much cooler than their equatorial position might indicate.

Every few years, disaster strikes this coast and its magnificently abundant population of birds: El Niño, a current of warm water originating off California, one relatively impoverished of minerals and therefore of plankton, strikes further south than usual. The west-coast climate ameliorates and the off-shore winds blow less vigorously, with the result that the upwelling ceases. As this happens, the warm Pacific water encroaches on to the coast and, with the anchovies migrating into deeper, cooler water, the bird communities

Little penguins in their nest chamber. The male feeds the chick, while the female adds straw to the nest. The access tunnel is behind the male's head. This photograph was taken from a hide built over the nest which was fitted with a removable hood (*John Warham*)

starve. Great is the mortality, and brown pelicans pitifully haunt the fish-markets of Lima for odd scraps which may prolong their lives for a day or two. Yet such is their fecundity that after the following breeding season when El Niño has returned, the populations are back to normal. The dependence of pelagic birds upon the vagaries of the ocean currents could not be more eloquently demonstrated. Penguin species range further up the west continental coasts than the east coasts simply because the regions of upwelling, of fertility, are found only on the west coasts.

The melting of the polar ice caps also influences the circulation and vertical mixing of the oceans, particularly in the southern hemisphere where the oceanographic details are best known. The effect of this on the distribution of sea birds can be clearly seen. Fresh water, being less dense, floats on top of brine. Therefore, as the Antarctic ice melts, the diluted water moves northwards towards the Equator. At the same time mineral-rich water from the oceanic abyss moves southwards and rises beneath the continental ice shelves, where it mixes to some extent with the surface water on its northward journey. The coasts of Antarctica are therefore abundant in plankton, particularly during the long days of spring and summer; but this area of plenty does not extend very far north, because when the rich, cool but light water of Antarctic origin meets the band of warm, sub-Antarctic seas, it sinks; this well-defined boundary of increased sea temperature is called the Antarctic Convergence.

In the South Atlantic the cool Antarctic water dips below the surface at about 50°S, and in turn the sub-Antarctic waters are superseded by the much warmer and less fertile equatorial water at 40°S, just north of Tristan da Cunha (the Sub-tropical Convergence). Cephalopods (squid) and flying fish are ten times more abundant in the surface waters beyond latitude 40°S, and crustacea about 10,000 times more numerous. It is within the Sub-tropical Convergence that the vast majority of penguins are to be found, and most of all within the fertile waters inside the Antarctic Convergence. A single hectare (2½ acres) near the Antarctic Convergence can produce 12,000kg (about 12 tons) of animal protein per year; that is more than twice as much as the very best pasture on the land.

The surface waters of the southern hemisphere can therefore be divided into tropical, sub-tropical, sub-Antarctic and Antarctic zones, and that these are of increasing productivity with increasing latitude is reflected in the zonal distribution of sea birds. On a journey southwards on the 20–30° west longitude, the relative frequency of sea-bird obser-

Brown Pelican

118

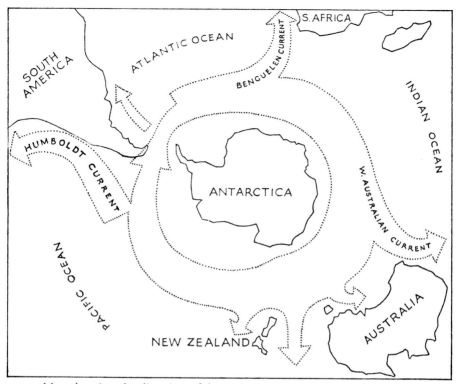

Map showing the direction of the main ocean currents
around Antarctica

vations were found to be four at 3° S, two at 22° S and no less
that twenty-seven at 55° S.

What exactly do penguins eat, and to what extent do the
diets vary from one species to another? King and emperor
penguins probably feed chiefly on squid, strong-swimming
molluscs which abound in the waters of Antarctica. One
taken from the stomach of an emperor measured 35–40cm
(13–15in) long, but fish and crustacea (in the form of shrimp-
like animals) are no doubt also taken to supplement the
molluscan diet.

Among the zooplankton, the floating and drifting animal
life within the Antarctic Convergence, the euphausid crustaceans are one of the most predominant, in particular one
species called *Euphausia superba*. Vast shoals of these shrimp-

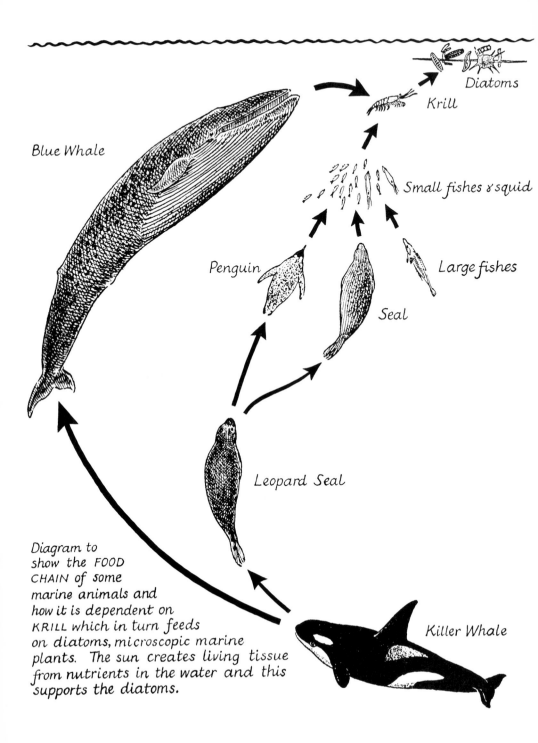

Diatoms

Krill

Blue Whale

Small fishes & squid

Penguin

Large fishes

Seal

Leopard Seal

Diagram to show the FOOD CHAIN of some marine animals and how it is dependent on KRILL which in turn feeds on diatoms, microscopic marine plants. The sun creates living tissue from nutrients in the water and this supports the diatoms.

Killer Whale

like creatures, grazing on the rich supply of diatoms, constitute the 'krill' upon which the great baleen whales feed. This krill is also the food of the smaller penguins, like adélies, gentoos, and chinstraps, all of which are characteristic birds of the Antarctic zones; the stomach of one gentoo held the remains of 960 euphausids, together with a number of pebbles. The excreta of these birds is often typically pink from the undigested remains of their crustacean meals, which are rich in vitamins and oils derived from the lush growth of diatoms.

Species sharing the same habitat do not generally compete for the same food, however, because otherwise one would tend to oust the others through inherent differences in hunting efficiency. As chinstraps, gentoos and rockhoppers may breed together and seek their food in the same areas, each species is probably adapted to taking a different proportion of the various kinds of food available, in much the same way as various species of auks do, when breeding together in the same loomeries. In the South Orkneys, chinstraps and adélies avoid unduly competing with each other by using different foraging ranges. Chinstraps tend to feed on adult krill around 90km (56 miles) from their rookeries, whereas adélies swim further afield, and tend to take juvenile krill. Perhaps connected with their preferred diet of smaller crustaceans, adélies breed a month earlier than their relatives. Similarly, gentoo and macaroni penguins at Bird Island, South Georgia tend to range 10 and 80km (6 and 50 miles) respectively from their rookeries in order to feed. Certainly rockhoppers at Cape Horn were found to have eaten a variety of animals, including fish and smaller species of crustacea (copepods and isopods), though crustaceans predominated and were apparently the chief food. Euphausid shrimps are much less numerous north of the Antarctic Convergence and rockhoppers on Tristan da Cunha make up for it by mainly eating squid; the stomach of a young one still being fed by the parents contained the remains of at least 369 individual squid.

Although magellanic penguins apparently hunt squid in the

A chinstrap penguin feeding its young (*Alfred Saunders*)

swirling giant kelp beds around Cape Horn, this and other Spheniscid penguins and the little penguin have a preference for fish. Unlike Antarctic waters, where pelagic shoaling fish are uncommon, the Benguelan and Humboldt Currents used to swarm with members of the herring family. In Southern Chile, magellanic penguins thrive on sardines, where as the more northerly Peruvians take mainly anchovetas, competing not only with the other guano-producing birds, but also with fishermen who see them as rivals.

In South Africa the activities of jackass penguins were for a long time seen as detrimental to commercial fishing interests. For this reason, several investigations were made to find out the seriousness of the avian threat. Twenty years ago, fish accounted for 94 per cent of the jackass' diet; 64 per cent by weight of this was pilchard, the remainder being made up by anchovy and maasbanker. A detailed analysis of the penguin's food revealed that 53 per cent was potentially fish destined for human consumption. The scale of the problem became all too clear. About 103,000 jackass penguins were breeding in the South West Cape Islands. At the height of their 185 day breeding season, each bird was catching the equivalent of 190 5cm (2in) long fish during each nine hour foraging trip. Over the course of the summer, this amounted to 7,000 tons, of which 2,900 tons was of economic importance to South Africa. Over the past two decades, there have been major changes in the fish populations, with a catastrophic decline in the stocks of pilchard. This has affected both fishermen and penguins alike. In the South Western Cape, the jackasses are now feeding mainly on anchovies.

Pilchards and anchovies are also important constituents in the diet of little penguins, although a further seventeen kinds of fish have been recorded in samples of their food. These they catch within 30km (18½ miles) of their rookeries in the comparatively shallow water over the coastal shelf.

The competition between the different species of the smaller penguins of the Antarctic zone, and between penguins and whales, for the vast but not inexhaustible supplies of krill may have vital bearing upon penguin numbers. The

123

Skuas stealing eggs from Adélie Penguin

Gentoo Penguin escaping from Leopard Seal

Giant Petrel taking young King Penguin

Sheathbill

Killer Whale chasing King Penguin

Predators of penguins

ruthlessly efficient whaling industry off South Georgia and the South Shetland Islands has removed a considerable slice of the whale population; indeed the hump-backed and the blue whale, two of the most magnificent products of evolution, and some of the most valuable animal commodities, have been all but exterminated in this shameful story of man's unabated greed. So the food which these whales would have eaten is now available to other animals. Dr W. J. Sladen has calculated that it could support no less than 300 million extra penguins! There is evidence that the chinstraps are in fact increasing in numbers on the edge of their range. For example, in Cooper Bay, South Georgia, sixty were reported in 1929, 300 in 1936, and 500 in 1947, an eightfold increase in twenty years. They have also extended their range eastwards in Antarctica recently, no longer being found only in the western and north-western sector; whether this is connected with the depletion of whale stocks is not known and in any case it is an unimpressive increase compared with the theoretical potential.

In their turn, penguins are preyed upon both on land and in the water, by a number of birds and mammals. Unfortunately, carnivorous predatory animals are considered by man to be murderers, plundering and terrifying the peaceful animal populations on which they feed; so in modern game practice a constant vigilance is exercised against many flesh-eating animals. Yet carnivores and scavengers, whether killer whales or lions, have a specific role to play in natural animal communities, culling the sickly or weak and thereby keeping the stock strong and their numbers in check, so that food supplies are not over-exploited. By removing a predator, man often upsets a relationship from which he profits. Lake Victoria in East Africa once contained many Nile crocodiles, which used to feed on worthless lung fish, which in turn preyed upon a commercially valuable fish, *Tilapia*. When the crocodiles were shot for their hides, and for lesser reasons, the lung fish population exploded, and the *Tilapia* catch *decreased*. Generally speaking, the numbers of the predators are strictly limited by the abundance of their prey.

125

The predatory skua or the leopard seal chasing a wretched adélie penguin around the ice floes should be considered as part of a mutually beneficial system which ensures that the maximum numbers of each kind can be allowed to live and reproduce. Indeed, every living organism has evolved by a process of selective mortality, some of which has been achieved by predation. A hungry leopard seal is merely *cropping*, not murdering penguins in much the same way as a cow is killing pieces of grass; only humans systematically slaughter their own or any other species.

On land, adult penguins are well-nigh invulnerable –

A sheathbill scavenging a rookery of chinstrap penguins (*Alfred Saunders*)

unless from introduced dogs – and so preying carnivores will tend to concentrate on the eggs and chicks. In the Antarctic, elephant seals sometimes damage adélie penguins by rolling over their nests in the course of moving through the rookeries; but this is only an incidental hazard. By far the most important Antarctic predator is the brown skua (*Catharacta skua lönnbergi*). The skua and the sheathbill are the only land-feeding birds on the Antarctic continent, possibly breeding as far south as the Danco Coast (lat 64° S) in West Graham Land. These gull-like scavengers – they have been called 'an enterprising firm of Antarctic dustmen' – will chase terns and gulls, swooping on the food they regurgitate.

In penguin rookeries Antarctic skuas may be seen taking unattended eggs, dropping the frozen ones to break them open. A brooding penguin can easily cope with one skua, but occasionally a pair will worry an incubating adélie, one threatening to attack from the front and the other from the rear, and by dividing the penguin's attentions one bird can sooner or later rush in and grab an egg. Feeding on newly-laid eggs is a messy business, because the albumen defies manipulation with the bill, and only the rich yolk can be picked up and swallowed. However, once the embryo is well developed the skuas can efficiently deal with the contents. Unguarded chicks are also quickly pounced upon, and again the parent's attention may be distracted so that its chick can be stolen.

Penguins do not of course remain indifferent to marauders, particularly in their own territory, and will chase the skuas with flailing flippers as though they truly intended to fly after them. At the same time, the skuas have adapted their behaviour to defeat the penguins' methods of defence; when attacking a wandering chick they will bowl it over and over until it comes to rest outside the perimeter of the rookery, where it can be killed without interference from adults. Should a victim manage to escape this initial buffeting it will run quickly for the crèche, where it will not be molested. Also the skuas will watch a sickly chick for several days, not striking until they know the youngster is too weak to

127

retaliate. This kind of surveillance does not necessarily indicate a real capacity for cunning, but skuas undoubtedly have come to recognize signs of ill-health or inexperience in their prey, and to associate these with an easily obtainable meal. Despite this, they do not find most of their food without effort; indeed, a rookery of about 100,000 adélie penguins can support only ten pairs of marauding scavengers.

The studies by Dr E. C. Young of South Polar skuas in an adélie rookery on Ross Island showed that far from being dependent on penguins for existence, the skuas could breed almost without having access to penguins; in any case, the breeding cycle of the skuas is behind that of the adélies, and as they are unable to kill adélie chicks of more than three weeks old, the rookeries cannot provide them with much live food after mid-January when their own chicks are becoming increasingly rapacious. The lack of synchronization of the two breeding cycles suggests that the skuas in this region are only exploiting one of a number of food sources. Furthermore, these birds are not specially adapted for feeding on penguins; their bills are not of carnivore shape, being only moderately suitable for gaining purchase on flesh, and the feet are poorly adapted for clutching, when compared with the talons of a falcon; nor is there any co-ordination between bill and feet as the skuas rip at a carcase.

The effects of skua depredations are not evenly felt over the whole of the rookery. Nests on the outskirts of the main breeding area, being relatively isolated, are more easily attacked by skuas, which are generally reluctant to enter the centres where every available piece of ground is vehemently protected by its owner. Furthermore, skuas tend to take more eggs and chicks from late-nesting adélies.

South Polar skuas tend not to worry emperor penguins, which to a large extent remain outside the range of these birds; but in the rookeries of the temperate regions, other species take their place. Gulls and ibises devour up to 40 per cent of the eggs of jackass penguins before they hatch, and scoreby's and dominican gulls rove sub-Antarctic rookeries.

Penguins of the low Antarctic are preyed upon by two

A sheathbill flying up and intercepting food which is being regurgitated by the chinstrap penguin for its chick (*Neville Jones, British Antarctic Survey*)

other birds: giant petrels and sheathbills. Giant petrels, related to albatrosses, are chiefly pelagic feeders, but in one rookery of king penguins they were the chief predators; probably most of the chicks they took were sickly and would anyhow have died an early death; although giant petrels are fairly adept at walking for members of their family, they can easily be outmanoeuvred by a healthy chick. In one breeding colony of giant petrels studied on Macquarie Island, the adults were disgorging 'bird intestines and penguin feet', besides cephalopods (squid), blubber and amphipod crustaceans; it was thought that the penguins were adults and were caught over the sea in the vicinity of the island. On the whole, though, the effect of giant petrels rarely reaches serious proportions.

Sheathbills (*Chionis* sp.) are, however, more widespread in Antarctica. These are peculiar, white, pigeon-like birds, related to the waders, and are found only in Antarctica, where they scavenge most of the southern rookeries. Sheathbills at Signy Island have been observed as adept at stealing poorly guarded young or eggs of chinstrap penguins and are suspected of killing very young ones. A large amount of excrement is also eaten, which must still contain a certain amount of nutritional material, useful at least for *Chionis*. Sheathbills depend most upon penguins during the season when both kinds of birds are feeding their young. The kind of roughage which adult sheathbills obtain from the shore during the year is not particularly suitable for their young, and so they take scraps of krill which have been inadvertently spilt on the ground by adult penguins in the process of feeding their chicks.

More remarkable is the way sheathbills intercept chinstrap parents engaged in regurgitating krill to their hungry young; as the parents start to transfer the food, the sheathbills fly up either between the two birds, or on to the back of the youngster who ducks; the regurgitated krill splashes on to the ground, to be grabbed by the thief. The sheathbill chicks grow well on this nourishing mixture of euphausid-shrimp remains, and there is evidence that should the supply be cut off they may lose weight, although some are reared in areas with no access to rookeries.

On Signy Island however, four out of the six breeding areas studied by Neville Jones of the British Antarctic Survey were associated with adélie and chinstrap rookeries. It cannot be stated that sheathbills inflict a heavy mortality on penguins; they may only have nuisance value. But at least on Signy Island the sheathbills are far more dependent on the

Jackass Penguin seeing off a gull from the vicinity of its nesting burrow.

rookeries as a source of food than are the skuas, and their breeding cycle is timed so that their chicks are most demanding when the penguins are passing large amounts of krill to their own chicks assembled in the crèches.

Swamp harrier, peregrine, white-bellied sea eagle, pacific gull, tiger snake, eastern water rat and blue-tongued lizard are all listed as predators of little penguins. Ferrets may represent something of a menace to yellow-eyed penguins in New Zealand, but of course until the colonization of these areas by man, penguins had no land-mammalian enemies. This is particularly true of Antarctica, where dogs have run riot and devastated rookeries of adélie penguins, and in 1951–52 their depredations ruined a population study of this species. Heavy mortalities were possible because the penguins have evolved no correctly orientated escape behaviour. Although so well adapted for life in the sea, all except possibly the nocturnal species of *Eudyptula* approach it with considerable reluctance. They will however leap on to *terra firma* without hesitation. This accounts for the tameness of most penguins, a trait which could lead to their downfall as surely as it has done for many flightless birds, should they be over-exploited or devastated by man or one of his introduced animals. There are some hopeful indications that penguins will learn to seek safety in the sea from marauding dogs.

It was a source of constant amusement to the early chroniclers of penguins to watch them line up on the shores near their rookeries waiting to enter the water. As more penguins jostled at the back of the group, one placed at the front would ultimately overbalance and dive into the sea below, its progress being keenly followed by all those left ashore. If all was well, they would quickly follow. This behaviour has a high survival value to those penguins which breed in the Antarctic zone, because the waters near the rookeries are the hunting grounds of the rapacious leopard seals, lithe, fast-swimming animals, with powerful jaws equipped with strong, sharp teeth. They hunt singly between the ice floes and lurk for unsuspecting penguins beneath the ledges from which they dive.

131

As a predator, the leopard seal probably has most effect on adélies, chinstraps, gentoos and rockhoppers, but it occasionally takes king or emperor penguins. During one breeding season 23·8 per cent of the chick-rearing king penguins in one rookery disappeared, and leopard seals may well have been responsible. One which was shot had no less than eighteen adélie penguins in its stomach and the digested remains of many more in its intestines. Since there are almost 100,000 of these animals off the Antarctic coasts, they must take a considerable toll of penguins over the course of a year. The method of catching a penguin is to give chase until the victim is exhausted, grab hold of it in the jaws and, with one flick of the head, separate the skin from the carcase which is swallowed whole; all that is left is the pelt floating on an oily patch of water. The whole incident is quickly over.

A fit penguin can usually outmanoeuvre a leopard seal and swim faster too. Although the seals may appear to choose their prey indiscriminately, it seems likely that they take chiefly young birds which have just come down to the sea or adults which are unhealthy or already injured. Young king penguins do not enter the water until spring, when leopard seals are less numerous around the coasts; it is for this reason that the breeding cycle of the king penguin has been prolonged to over a year. In the southern autumn the seas are patrolled by leopard seals, so the young undergo a winter's fast and go to sea in the following spring, with correspondingly increased chances of survival.

Fur seals (*Gypophoca tasmanica*) may poach adult little penguins off the Australian coast. Killer whales, which hunt in packs, also take occasional penguins, particularly the larger emperors, but for them penguins are trivial morsels compared with seals – their main prey.

Leopard Seal and Chinstrap Penguin

(*above*) King penguins have an incubation period of nearly eight weeks, their breeding cycle takes up to fifteen months to complete, so they only breed twice in every three years (*Wolfgang Kaehler*)

(*below*) Magellanic penguins at the burrow entrances of a rookery at Punta Tombo, Argentina (*Gunter Ziesler, Bruce Coleman Ltd*)

Penguins meet their worst dangers during their pre-adult phase. Once they have achieved maturity they can expect to live for many years. A king penguin in Edinburgh Zoo lived to be at least twenty-eight years old, but of course the length of survival in captivity does not necessarily show what ages are customarily achieved in the rough-and-tumble of natural conditions. Some yellow-eyed penguins certainly reach at least twenty-two years of age in their own environment, although the average may be between six and eight years. A chinstrap penguin which was ringed as a young bird by the British Antarctic Survey was at least fifteen years old when last seen in November 1963, after which observations at the rookery ceased.

Broadly, the number of young recruited into the breeding population must balance the adults lost. As adult penguins are reasonably long-lived, with a low mortality rate, the pre-adult mortality must be correspondingly high. The overall survival rate of chicks will vary from one rookery to another; only 18 per cent of adélie penguin chicks reach the crèche stage in some rookeries, and of these only a small proportion will reach maturity; at Cape Royds 50 per cent of the chicks managed to reach the sea but the weather conditions may have been particularly favourable. There may be a 90 per cent mortality of emperor penguin chicks. In yellow-eyed penguins, 21 per cent of the chicks die before reaching seven weeks of age – much of this mortality being due to the parents inadvertently crushing them! The overall annual mortality among adults of this species has been estimated by L. E. Richdale as 13 per cent; therefore, as the population remains stable, there is only room for an annual increment of this proportion to the breeding population. A colony of 1,100 birds raises 399 juveniles, of which 152 remain after four months, 129 after two years, and 108 survive their third year to make good adult mortality. Much of this loss occurs at sea,

(above) Adélie chicks are fed on krill by regurgitation (*Wolfgang Kaehler*)

(below) Mutual preening by the sub-antarctic royal penguins, Macquarie Island, New Zealand (*Wolfgang Kaehler*)

when the young are competing for food with the more experienced and less vulnerable adults. A pair of breeding penguins, because of their long life expectancy, may take many seasons to rear two chicks to adulthood to replace themselves in the population.

Penguin populations must now cope with another source of mortality. Civilized man has been the penguins' most dangerous enemy. In South America, members of the Alacaluf and Yahgan tribes have probably raided rookeries and have taken gentoo, king, rockhopper, peruvian and magellanic penguins and their eggs from time immemorial, but here the relationship was one of hunter and hunted at a non-exploitive level; predation was limited and it seems unlikely that the populations of birds suffered. Similarly, the Maoris of New Zealand killed albatrosses and sooty petrels and probably also penguins; they preserved the young birds in fat protected by algae fronds, and the food was then called *hua hua*. Then, in the fifteenth century European man entered the southern seas, and, as described in Chapter 7, in the next 450 years pillaged penguins on an unprecedented scale.

To what extent is man a serious menace to penguins today? On the west coasts of South America, he certainly conflicts with them. Eggs are still collected from *Spheniscus* rookeries, and the removal of large amounts of guano and top soil from the islands where they breed prevents the birds from making burrows. Consequently, they nest on the surface, where they may be more prone to aerial predators and over-exposure to the sun. There is evidence that the ever-increasing annual harvest of anchovies by man is reducing their food supplies, which must have a profound effect upon the populations not only of magallanic, peruvian and jackass penguins, but also of the other species of sea birds which eat these fish.

It is in the sub-Antarctic and Antarctic regions where the numbers of penguins are greatest that rookeries have been most heavily culled in the past, particularly near South Georgia. Some of the finest penguin rookeries were relatively undisturbed until recently. With increasing interest in polar research and the consequent expansion of scientific activity in

Peruvian Penguins

the Antarctic, rookeries have been extensively studied, and it is becoming apparent that the balance of life in this region is always precarious. This is due to the uniquely severe climate and the fact that the mammalian and avian fauna depends exclusively on the sea for its food. Frosts and heavy snowfalls may block up the leads to the sea, compelling the animals relying upon them to forgo food or expend much more energy in obtaining it. Studies of the breeding success of the indigenous Antarctic birds show that chick mortality is very high when compared with that of many temperate species and unsuccessful annual cycles are more normal than exceptional. One study of wilson's petrel showed a regular chick mortality of 65 per cent, though no evidence of adult mortality; and virus infections have been known to kill off 85 per cent of the young crab-eater seals.

In this already difficult environment, the presence of man, with his infinite capacity for creating waste and spreading contamination – in the form of toxic chemicals, which have recently turned up even in Antarctica – for disturbing and for killing, may tip the delicately balanced ecological set-up towards destruction. That this is no alarmist pipedream is illustrated by the way some rookeries of adélie penguins have started to contract because of disturbance by man. The one at Cape Royds contained 2,000 pairs in 1956, but by December 1961 only 1,250 pairs were counted, and this reduction was thought to be due to incubating birds being disturbed by visiting personnel to Antarctica, all of whom express interest in seeing a penguin city. This is happening all over Antarctica; an example of the kind of disturbance inadvertently created is described in Chapter 6.

Scientists are increasingly visiting and working in rookeries and duplicating research, but if this is going to be to the detriment of their objects of study then their movements and activities will have to be more rigidly controlled. Constant surveillance of Antarctica with helicopters and the increased logistic capability of that continent means ever-increasing disturbance of penguins by aeroplane. Prospects for increasing tourism within Antarctica should be viewed

with concern, and the visitors orchestrated with care and sympathy for the fragile environment.

A further development may also have far-reaching repercussions on the fauna of Antarctica: the large-scale harvesting of krill in the South Polar waters. A rapid increase of food will be required for the booming population of man, and developments in methods of harvesting plankton have brought krill fishing to commercial levels. In Antarctica nearly everything depends ultimately on krill, and any removal of this large scale source of food must result in a disturbance of the region's bio-economics.

However, species like adélie penguins are still numerous, so why does conservation need discussion? R. C. Murphy pointed out some time ago the fallacy of the argument that a species is in no danger because it is still common. Who would have thought a decade or two ago that many species of whales could have been brought to the brink of extinction? Old accounts tell us of the sea in some parts of the world almost broiling with whales and the air used to be heavy with the oily tang of their breath – in regions which never see a whale now from year to year. The disappearance of the American passenger pigeon offers another salutary warning against complacency.

It was to meet these dangers that the Scientific Committee for Antarctic Research, at its fifth meeting in October 1961, proposed that selected areas should be designated as permanent sanctuaries. The first steps would be to request the dozen or so governments taking part in research there to bring their regulations into harmony with the recommendations I–VIII of the First Antarctic Treaty Consultative Meeting at Canberra. In short, recognition was given to the need to conserve the living resources of the treaty area. Further recommendations were expressed subsequently but unfortunately the Treaty area does not cover any areas north of 60° S, or the high seas. The existence of SCAR and the declaration by the treaty powers of an area of scientific cooperation ought to give the wild life of this region a chance of rational conservation, despite the many problems involved.

Not many of the temperate and sub-tropical species stand in much danger at the moment, although the peruvian and magellanic and possibly the jackass penguins may be threatened in the near future directly through the activities of man.

The original 'penguin', the great auk, was still common in the waters of the north Atlantic 200 years ago, and it was ruthlessly driven into extinction by 250 years of unrelenting persecution. We have some reason for hope that the birds which now bear the name will not share its fate.

5 · The Evolution of Penguins

We have already dealt with the life history of penguins, a life described admirably half a century ago by a chronicler of penguins as one devoted to feeding, fighting, courting, thieving and philandering. But penguins have another life, and one which is no less interesting: an evolutionary life, embracing all those imperceptibly slow changes which have culminated in the penguins we know today. They can only be deduced from the fossils and from comparing the anatomy of a range of present day birds. From these sources, a history can be surmised which may help to establish the penguin's place in the fabric of life on earth.

However, it must be recorded that the penguin's family roots are shrouded in some mystery because no fossil penguin more than 45 million years old has yet been unearthed. By then, flying birds, essentially similar to those we know today were already well established. Furthermore, those scraps of ancient skeletal debris have all been discovered within the present day range of penguins; the most southerly fossil materialized on the Antarctic Peninsula at 64° 15′ S, and the most northerly, near Adelaide, Australia.

It was the great nineteenth-century zoologist Thomas Henry Huxley who first brought fossil penguins to the attention of scientists, and he named altogether thirty-five species included in twenty-five *genera*, deduced from fragments of bone. Any study into the evolutionary history of

The Miocene fossil penguin (*Pachydyptes ponderosus*) shown in comparison with a man and two modern penguins, the Emperor and Little

animal families is almost bound to yield giant species, and penguins are no exception. In 1905 and 1930 remains of penguins much larger than extant forms were discovered in New Zealand and on Seymour Island, in rocks which were laid down in the Miocene period anything between 11–25 million years ago. The birds of which these were the remnants were subsequently named *Pachydyptes ponderosus* and *Anthropornis nordenskjöldi* – *Pachydyptes* means heavy diver and *Anthropornis*, man bird. The sizes of these two mega-penguins were greatly exaggerated in popular writings, which suggested that there once lived penguins as large as men or even 2m (7ft) tall; so there may have been, but their remains elude us. The most impressive one was probably *Anthropornis*, which might have stood tall at between 1·52 and 1·7m (60–70in); *Pachydyptes* was less imposing at about 1·37–1·52m (54–60in). For comparison, the emperor, our largest surviving penguin, stands about 1·06m (42in) high and weighs about 30kg (60lb). The two extinct species might have tipped the scales at 90–135kg (198–298lb) – each as heavy as a substantially overweight man. Since penguins can be very pugnacious, and determined in pressing home vigorous flippering attacks, such heavyweights would have been best given a wide berth, at least, around their nest sites. *Pachydyptes* and *Anthropornis* are known only from humeri (flipper bones) and tarsometatarsi (leg bones) respectively, scant remains indeed; their vital statistics have therefore been computed with the help of a formula derived from a study of all modern species, which it has been assumed can be applied also to the extinct ones. The relationship between the length of the limb bones and the length of the penguins can be expressed as:

Total length of penguin = tarso-metatarsal length multiplied by a factor varying from 18½ to 24

or

Total length of penguin = femoral length multiplied by a factor varying from 8½ to 9½.

Five to ten per cent is deducted from the total length of the penguin to obtain the standing height.

By substituting in these equations we can arrive at the approximate figure quoted for the standing height of *Pachydyptes* and *Anthropornis*. The skeletons of so many of the larger extinct birds have been carefully built up from isolated bones, but these two giants remain as figures on a piece of paper. What is certain is that they did not survive beyond the Miocene period. Perhaps they lost out in competition with the smaller whales and seals, two groups of marine mammals which were in the ascendance at the time. Another three known fossil species stood higher than the emperor, the largest extant kind, but the vast majority of all the penguin species which have ever lived have more closely approximated in size to contemporary ones.

The key to the origin and relationship of penguins has always been connected with their inability to fly. Is it possible that the ancestors of penguins were themselves non-volant? Or have penguins evolved from flying birds, having secondarily given up aerial for underwater flight? Zoologists pondered these questions for nearly a century before satisfactory answers were forthcoming.

In order to appreciate the various theories which have been put forward about the origin of penguins, it is necessary to outline briefly the evolutionary history of birds in general. Most responsible biologists agree that the many different kinds of living things have been produced by descent, with modification, from previously existing forms – not by being created separately by special ordinance. This briefly is what Darwin's theory of evolution is all about. The changes involved in the gradual evolution of a species can often be traced back through the fossil record, with the most recent fossils showing the greatest similarity to extant forms. The number of fossilized remains of primitive birds in particular get progressively fewer farther back in the geological record. Only one fossil species from the Jurassic age, of 140 million years ago, has come to light: in 1861, at Langenaltheimer Haardt, near Pappenheim, in Bavaria, a block of fine-grained limestone was split open during quarrying operations to reveal a well-preserved skeleton, with feather impressions of

Millions of years		
– 1	PLEISTOCENE	*Man*
– 10	PLIOCENE	
– 20	MIOCENE	*Nuthatch* A passerine from lower Pliocene. Earliest fossil found in Italy.
– 30	OLIGOCENE	*Proconsul* A primitive anthropoid ape, abundant in E. Africa in early Miocene, close to the common stock from which great apes and man arose.
– 40		
– 50	EOCENE	*Albatross* The earliest known albatross (Gigantornis) had a 20' wing span.
– 60	PALEOCENE	*Penguin* The earliest fossil Penguin was found in New Zealand. The giant penguins appeared later in the Miocene period.
– 70		
– 80		
– 90		*Hesperornis* A large, flightless, swimming sea bird, which resembled present day loons.
– 100	CRETACEOUS	
– 110		*Dinosaur* Stegosaurus, a 30' long heavily armoured, herbivorous dinosaur.
– 120		
– 130		
– 140		*Archaeopteryx* The first known bird, about the size of a Magpie. A perfect mosaic of reptilian and avian characters.
– 150		
– 160	JURASSIC	*Plesiosaur* A 20' long reptile, re-adapted to live in water.
– 170		
– 180		
– 190	TRIASSIC	*Euparkeria* A 3' long bi-pedal reptile, related to ancestors of birds.
– 200		

Table showing the Geological Periods during the last 200 million years

a bird which was subsequently named as *Archaeopteryx lithographica*. It was crow-sized, had teeth, a long whip-like tail, and no keel on its breast bone; but because of the impressions of feathers (well-formed primaries and secondaries), it was undoubtedly a *bird*, although a fairly primitive prototype even by Cretaceous standards.

No more clues about earlier stages in bird history have been yielded. Where, therefore do we look for the real pro-avian stock? The skull and other bone structures of *Archaeopteryx* make it fairly clear that the ancestors of birds were reptiles, and the ones that most nearly fit the bill were a family of small lizard-like animals which skipped along on their hind legs. These have been named Pseudosuchians. Their remains have been found in Germany, Scotland and South Africa, so they must have been quite widespread in the Triassic era, about 200 million years ago, when the Age of Reptiles was just about getting under way – and some 30–60 million years or so before the skies became dotted with flying reptiles (pterodactyls) and birds.

We can only surmise the circumstances that gave flight such a great survival value to an evolving stock of bipedal Pseudosuchians; they were in any case responsible for seeding and maintaining the branch that led to birds. There may have been overcrowding and competition for living space on the ground, so that animals which sought their food in the trees where insect life may have been prodigious and as yet untapped, could have had the advantage over their terrestrial competitors. A bipedal habit involves the ability to balance, and could have been an asset for running along branches; and possibly the forearms would have been used for grasping and to help in balancing. From here, there may have been a gradual development from branch-jumping to gliding from tree to tree, or from tree to ground, in terms of escaping from enemies, this behaviour would have been invaluable. Feathers may have evolved concomitantly with flight, which would have been greatly improved by their elongation on the forearm to act as an aero foil. Elaboration of the muscles actuating the wings, and the necessary development of a strong breastbone for their attachment, together with a few other changes, would almost have produced the birds we know today.

The view that all modern birds are descendants of these first flying birds, which looked like *Archaeopteryx*, has not always been held. In 1887, a theory was put forward by M. A. Menzbier that penguins had gradually evolved from reptiles independently of other birds. Though upright, aquatic and flightless animals, they possess many features in common with other birds (e.g. feathers) and they were thought to be an example of convergent evolution; in other words, Menzbier thought that similar features had been developed quite independently in unrelated evolving groups, and that therefore birds were polyphyletic – not a homogeneous group with the same ancestry. Menzbier argued that if this was the case the penguin's flipper was not a modified *wing*, but a direct adaptation of a reptilian fore-limb for underwater use; it had not evolved through a flying stage.

The controversy about the origin of the flipper featured in a later theory elaborated by another zoologist, P. R. Lowe, in 1933. He did not go so far as to suggest that penguins had taken their own evolutionary path from reptiles, but he doubted whether they had ever been through a flying stage; though sharing a common line of descent with other birds, they must have broken clear at an early stage, before flight had evolved. Evidence from various fields of work was used to support this. Lowe thought that the bone structure of the legs was closer to that of small, running dinosaurs. The embryological development of an animal is often thought to retrace its evolutionary history, and Lowe was quick to point out that penguin embryos seem to sport flippers and not wings right from the first stage in their early development.

This argument has been applied to the various families of flightless birds, the ostrich, rhea, cassowary, emu and kiwi. They have been called *ratites* as opposed to *carinates* because of their flat, raft-like breastbone. Some people have held the view that the ratites were a primitive group descended from birds that had never evolved the powers of flight, and

Archaeopteryx inherited a long tail from its lizard-like ancestors. In modern birds the terminal series of tail bones has become fused into the PYGOSTYLE which supports a fan of tail feathers. In Penguins this indicates flying ancestors.

Pygostyle of Adélie Penguin

147

therefore ratites were themselves more primitive than flying birds. For this reason they were classified apart from other birds in a super-order called the Palaeognathae. However, attractive though Lowe's theory may have been, evidence has accumulated over the years to prove that the penguins' ancestors were volant.

This fact is indeed indelibly stamped on a penguin's structure. The flipper is constructed as a paddle-like modification of a flying wing, showing the fusion of the carpal and metacarpal bones (the equivalent of man's wrist and hand

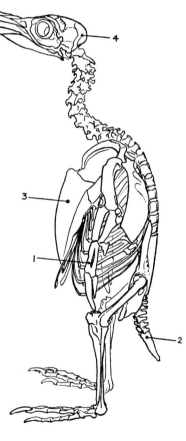

The skeleton of a penguin, (Eudyptes sp.) showing how certain features associated with flight are incorporated into the penguin's structure and therefore betray its flying ancestry.

1. Carpo metacarpus. Some carpals (wrist bones) fuse to the metacarpals to produce this structure. It is better able to withstand the stresses imposed by flight - when the ancestors of penguins were flying birds.
2. Pygostyle. Formed by the fusion of caudal vertebrae for the attachment of tail feathers.
3. Keeled sternum for the attachment of the strong muscles working the flippers.
4. Skull enveloping a brain with features adapted to flight.

Wing bones of a goose to compare with those of a penguin on the facing page.

148

bones) to form the carpo-metacarpus; this is a modification to strengthen the wing for the attachment of quills – so necessary for supporting flight – though the quills have long since been lost by penguins. The breastbone too shows features similar to those found in flying birds. The breastbone of *Archaeopteryx*, of undoubted flying or gliding capability, was more like that of the terrestrial Pseudosuchians from which it had evolved than that of the terrestrial penguins; for example, a penguin's breastbone is strongly keeled for anchoring the powerful pectoral and supracoracoideus muscles developed initially for flying.

Perhaps the most convincing evidence of aerial ancestry is the presence of a small bony structure called the pygostyle, which supports the tail feathers. *Archaeopteryx* inherited a long whip-like tail, supported by twenty or so vertebrae, from its lizard-like ancestors, and on it the feathers were arranged laterally in pairs. In the interests of aerodynamic efficiency and manoeuvrability the terminal series of tail bones became abbreviated, and some fused into a small knob of bone – the pygostyle. This adaptation to flight came to support a fan-like arrangement of tail feathers, and is found in all modern birds; for penguins, it must be an evolutionary hangover from flying ancestors.

Another small clue is that penguins sleep with the bill tucked behind the flipper – a posture that has some relevance to birds with properly developed wings and scapular feathers that all but cover the head when sleeping; in these flightless creatures, the stance seems inappropriate and merely a legacy from volant ancestors.

Penguins also have a very elaborate and highly developed cerebellum, that part of the brain discussed in Chapter 1 as being concerned with making the rapid adjustments and co-ordination of muscular action required by flying birds, reacting to the information coming in from the balance organs of the middle ears. This cerebellum, too, is a legacy from aerial progenitors.

Early theories about which birds were most closely related to penguins were as diverse as they were improbable. The

Partial dissection of the underside of an Adélie's flipper, showing the broad, flat bones.

149

popular confusion between them and the auks is reflected by the origin of the name penguin, which was first applied to the flightless great auk, the most penguin-like of all the auks. Ducks and geese were also thought to be near relations, but perhaps the most romantic suggestion was that penguins were allies of the elephant birds, large flightless creatures (order *Aepyornithiformes*) confined to Madagascar. The elephant birds' chief claim to fame, however, was that they were probably responsible for inspiring the Arab legends of the Ruhk or Roc of Sinbad the Sailor and Marco Polo. The largest species probably stood over 3·5m (10ft) high, although the majority were smaller; fossilized eggs buried during the Pleistocene era, some 1–2 million years ago, are still washed up on those shores.

A much more plausible idea, put forward in 1888 by a zoologist called Fürbinger, was that the penguins have a greater affinity to the tubenoses (*Procellariiformes*). This order includes the albatrosses, fulmars, petrels, diving petrels and shearwaters; fate has taken a queer turn if the earth-bound penguins have as their nearest relatives a group of species which soar with unsurpassed skill over the oceans according to the vagaries of the winds. Yet Fürbinger's theory is generally held today in ornithological circles, despite the fact that recent work by Professor Charles Sibley, Curator of Birds, Cornell University, on the egg-white proteins of penguins and of six species of tubenoses does not confirm the relationship. The basis for this work is that the egg-whites of closely related species have a similar chemical constitution, and that differences tend to increase as the birds become further apart on the avian family tree. Of course, the separation of the penguins (*Sphenisciformes*) from the tubenoses probably occurred something like 100 million years ago, and certainly the penguins which lived 20 million years ago were in many respects similar to modern ones; as Professor Sibley points out, it would perhaps be surprising if

In the breeding season magellanic penguins hunt the inshore kelp beds for squid and cuttlefish (*Ronald Templeton, Oxford Scientific Films*)

150

penguins and tubenoses had not diverged in their protein structure, and in other ways, over such a long period of independent history.

Fossil evidence fairly convincingly endorses the suspected affinity of tubenoses and penguins. One of the oldest penguin skulls, discovered in Patagonia in 1933, shows some rather primitive characteristics although it is reckoned to be only about 25 million years old and a lot younger than the most ancient of penguin fossils. Certain aspects of its design, together with the structure of older fossilized tarsometatarsal bones, have been interpreted as primitive and clearly bear some resemblance to the corresponding bones of tubenoses, the family that includes the albatrosses, shearwaters, petrels and fulmars.

Birds hand down stereotyped behaviour in the form of courtship displays from generation to generation largely by genetical means – much as a structural characteristic is passed on – and therefore an analysis of bird rituals can sometimes help elucidate relationships. Albatrosses in their nesting grounds will, during their mutual displays or dances, throw back the head and hold the wings at right angles to the body – the basic conformation adopted in the penguin's Ecstatic display. And both albatrosses and penguins may use stones or nest material in their courtship ceremonies. However, as a tool for classifying birds or animals, comparative behaviour studies should be used carefully: like anatomical features, ritual may be highly adaptive, and species perhaps totally unrelated may have evolved similar behaviour patterns which have survival value in environments that share certain characteristics. For example, swifts and emperor penguins may both huddle for warmth, and yet no one would seriously suggest that the two species are closely related; among the

(*above*) Gentoo penguins on sea ice; their distribution is circumpolar (*Doug Allan, Oxford Scientific Films*)

(*below*) Little or fairy penguins coming ashore under cover of darkness, a tourist spectacle on Phillip Island, off the coast of Australia (*Photo Library of Australia*)

The courtship display of the Wandering Albatross
(From a photograph by Rankin 1951)

Display in the Peruvian Penguin

smaller perching birds, those which breed in a particular habitat may build similar, and often complex, types of nests, which help to combat certain kinds of predators, although the builders may be entirely unrelated.

But even if the similarity of ritual is discounted, the tubenoses look as convincing a group as any other for sharing a common ancestor with the penguins perhaps 100 million years ago: they are primarily oceanic, many are burrow nesters, and they have long maturation periods comparable with those of penguins. Also the young of members of the penguin genus *Eudyptula* (i.e. the little and white-flippered), considered to be the most primitive of all penguins, develop tube-like openings in their nostrils reminiscent of the structure found in adult tubenoses.

So, some 100 million years ago, perhaps during the Upper Cretaceous period when chalk was being slowly sedimented in the warm, shallow seas around our coasts, the ancestors of today's penguins were shearwater-like birds, traversing the oceans. During the next 30 million years, they lost their ability to fly and emerged as penguins – a little different in structure from modern ones, but unmistakably penguins. Needless to say, the jump they made was a big one, and we can only conjecture the steps by which that change took place.

Shearwaters are beautifully adapted to flying from one wave trough to another and penguins are similarly adapted to flying under water in pursuit of their food. A bird in process of evolving from one of these types of organization to the other would be correspondingly less well adapted for flying on the one hand, and for sub-aqua flight on the other. When faced with competition from flying and non-flying forms, the bird which was intermediate in structure and habit would be at a disadvantage. It is for this reason that natural selection may operate more fiercely with intermediates, and that evolution, advancing in a series of steps, will linger much longer on some than others. Because of this, fossils of 'missing links' are rare, and none have been found to indicate evolutionary stages of penguins.

155

Consideraton of present-day species may yield some clues to form a coherent story. Here the petrel order, from which penguins probably evolved, is important because it contains a group of birds which effectively live as penguins for some of the year. These are the diving petrels, of which there are four species, all living in the colder parts of the oceans of the southern hemisphere (family Pelecanoididae). Blackish above and whitish below, they resemble to some extent the smaller Arctic auks, and in particular the doveky or little auk; the suggestion that the diving petrels were in fact really members of the auk family has, however, been discredited: the similarity between these inhabitants of the different Poles is due to the process of convergent evolution. The diving petrels assemble in flocks at sea, where they seek their food by flying under water; they breed in burrows on the sub-Antarctic islands; and like little penguins they feed their young chiefly at night.

The most significant point about the diving petrels is that

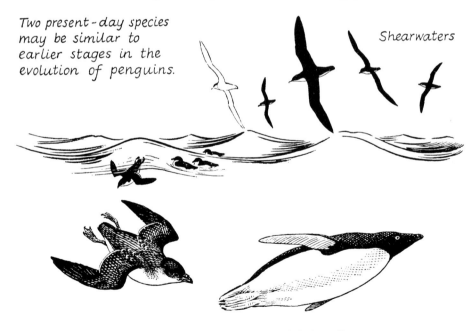

Two present-day species may be similar to earlier stages in the evolution of penguins.

Shearwaters

Diving Petrels

Adélie Penguin

they moult their quills all at once while at sea outside the breeding season. Loss of flight feathers of course leaves the birds flightless; but they can still fly very well beneath the water, and aerial flight is only required for the annual return to the islands where they breed. The diving petrels then are almost 'pre-adapted penguins', at least during the period when they are growing new wing feathers, and they could represent a stage through which the ancestors of penguins passed. As explained in Chapter 1, the requirements for a wing adapted for aerial flight and one adapted for use under water are quite different, and to some extent are incompatible; for large-sized birds, a wing big enough to support aerial flight would be too large and clumsy, and insufficiently strong, for underwater use.

The evolutionary history of penguins can be seen as an account of the gradual perfection of flight beneath the surface. A bird perhaps rather similar to a modern shearwater, with its ability to use the winds over the seas but with less efficiency under water, reached a stage resembling that of today's diving petrels, where the advantages to be gained by perfecting underwater flight, using the wings for propulsion, were much greater than those conferred by maintaining powers of aerial flight. In these conditions, if the appropriate genetic variations existed, then the powers of flight would gradually be lost. This evolutionary process culminated in the development of the flipper, so ideally suitable for propelling penguins through the sea as they hunt down their food or move to their rookeries. The flipper, then, never really ceased to be a wing, simply changing its medium of operation.

It is not suggested, of course, that penguins have evolved from shearwaters or diving petrels as we know them today, but that these may represent stages through which they have passed. Indeed, the geological evidence suggests that the diving petrels may be a relatively young group, as the only fossil comes from the Pleistocene period, a mere two million years ago. Possibly the tubenose group is once again following an evolutionary path leading to the development of penguin-like birds!

The reason for the restriction of penguins to the oceans south of the Equator (with the exception of the galapagos penguin), is to be found in their evolutionary history. Their progenitors, the tubenoses, also evolved in regions south of the Equator, although they have since extended their range to cover all the oceans of the world. As a family, penguins are chiefly inhabitants of the temperate regions – as, from the fossil distribution, they were in the Miocene era. Even today, seven species are temperate in their distribution, and a further four could be considered sub-tropical. Only two, the adélie and emperor, spend their lives entirely within the Antarctic circle, a further five living in areas bathed by the cool currents emanating from there. From the relatively warm regions, then, they have penetrated to both north and south.

Why have they not penetrated just a little further, into the northern hemisphere? The answer seems to be that penguins cannot tolerate tropical warm water. The line of the extreme northern limit of their range coincides nicely with the line linking places with a mean annual *air* temperature of 20°C (68°F) – which in turn is reflected by the oceanic currents and their temperatures. It seems that having evolved in the temperate waters of the southern hemisphere they have been trapped there, the warm equatorial waters and high air temperatures to the north effectively forming a physical barrier through which they were unable to swim; they have had to keep to regions which are bathed by the relatively cool water derived from the melting ice of Antarctica or regions of upwelling of cool abyssal water. The cool water of the Humboldt current is particularly strong, surging up to the Equator, bathing the equatorial Galapagos Islands, which as already mentioned have in spite of their position a relatively temperate climate in which the most northerly penguin species thrives.

So far as can be judged, habitats in the North Atlantic and Pacific would have been ideal for penguins, although of course there would have been competition from auks for the available food supply and nesting sites. In the Miocene era there was indeed a large flightless auk (*Mancalla*), and the

158

recent extinction of the great auk has left a vacant niche in the North Atlantic which could theoretically be filled by a penguin species. Of course the problems of introducing and establishing a new species are formidable, as the 1936 introduction into Norway has shown. In October that year, nine king penguins were released at Röst, Lofoten, Gjesvaer and in Finnmark, by Carl Schøyen of the Nature Protection Society. Two years later a number of macaroni and jackass penguins joined them under the auspices of the National Federation for the Protection of Nature.

The reasons for the liberation are not altogether clear, and the results were not entirely happy. The local people were not prepared for such exotic additions to the fauna and several kings met an ignominious end; one, when found to be moulting, looked so miserable that it was quickly dispatched; another was promptly put down by a woman who thought it was a bogey. In 1944 another met its end on a fisherman's hook set at a depth of between 6 and 15m (6½–16½yd); it was otherwise in good condition, and as it weighed about 4·2kg (9¼lb), was probably a macaroni. Many observers were convinced of the return of the great auk, and reports came through until 2 July 1954, when a single bird of unknown species was seen at Selsøyodden, outside Kyllingmark in Hamarøy.

Although some of these introduced penguins survived for perhaps eighteen years, there were no records of them attempting to nest. It is certain, however, that the climate in this part of the world is conducive to successful breeding once the birds have become synchronized to our winter-summer regime. Edinburgh Zoo has since 1919 built up an enviable record of breeding the sub-Antarctic penguins in outside pens; among their most notable successes have been kings – which they now export – gentoos, chinstaps and macaronis.

6 · Discovery

In the middle of the seventh century AD, the canoe *Te-Ivi-o-Atea*, with a crew of Polynesians under the command of Uite-'Rangiora, sailed as far south as the 'frozen ocean' off the Antarctic continent. We cannot be sure how far they went, but there is little doubt that they must have seen Antarctic penguins in their home waters, and perhaps they were the first to do so. Certainly they would have welcomed the birds as fresh food. The indigenous natives of New Zealand, South Africa and southern South America knew and used penguins as an important source of meat, oil and skins; yet in the northern hemisphere no European even knew of their existence.

In the early years of the fifteenth century the European world scarcely extended beyond the Mediterranean and as far south as the Canary Islands. But while the British showed little enthusiasm, the Spanish and Portuguese explorers put to sea and pioneered routes round the coasts of Africa and to the East, and across the Atlantic to the West Indies and the South American continent. So who was the first European ever to see a penguin, and when? Without much doubt it was a

Spaniard or a Portuguese. The earliest written reference is possibly in a manuscript account of the voyage of Vasco da Gama to India in 1499. An anonymous writer on board the *Angrade Sao Bras* saw birds 'as large as ganders and with a cry resembling the braying of asses, which could not fly' off the South African coast. Jackass penguins: the Portuguese called them *Sotylicayros*, a name they also used for the northern family of auks, birds which have a superficial resemblance to penguins.

The earliest certain record of South American penguins seems to be that of Antonio Pigafetta, an Italian scholar who sailed with Magellan in 1519, in the carrack *Trinidada* (11 burthen, 78ft/24m LWL). During the course of their epic circumnavigation, they discovered the now-famous Magellan Strait between Tierra del Fuego and the Patagonian coast. Pigafetta writes in his log of huge flocks of 'strange geese'. Later entries describe these strange geese as penguins, in entries such as 'Thus following this (Patagonian) coast towards the Pole Antartike, they came to a place where were two islands replenished with Penguins and Seales, the Penguins being all of blacke colour, and such as cannot flye.'

The name penguin – not recorded in English before 1588, according to the *Oxford English Dictionary* – was probably originally given by Spanish sailors to the short-winged northern auks and divers, from the quantity of fat (*penguigo*) found on them. But the name could also derive from the Latin *pinguis*, fat. Again, in 1575 Manuel de Mesquitor Perestrello speaks of the fine down at the ends of the wings as *penugen*, a name close to the modern Portuguese *pinguin*. There is a Welsh claim that the name penguin comes from two old Welsh words meaning 'white head' and originally referring to the now-extinct great auk. In the third volume of *Hakluyt's Voyages* there is an account by Sir Humfrey Gilbert, Knight, of

> a noble and worthy personage, lineally descended from the blood-royall borne in Wales, named Madock ap Owen Gwyneth, who, departing from the coast of England, about the yeare of our Lord God 1170, arrived and planted himself and his colonies [in

161

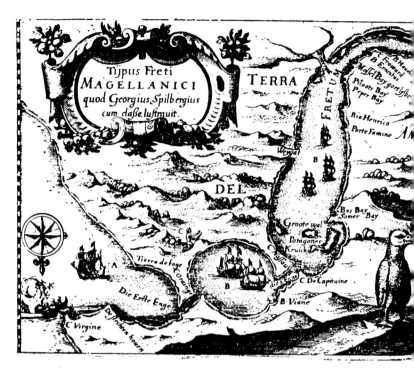

Newfoundland] and afterword returned himself into England, leaving certain of his people there, as appeareth in an ancient Welsh Chronicle, where he then gave to certaine Islands, beasts and foules, sundry Welsh names, as the Island of Penguin, which yet to this day beareth the same. There is likewise a foule in the saide countreys called by the same name as this day, and is as much to say in English, as Whitehead, and in trueth the said foules have white heads.

The flightless, penguin-like, but northern great auk did indeed have a white eye-patch, and what more natural than that sailors should transfer their name for the great auk to superficially similar birds in the south. But though the Welsh might well have a claim on Newfoundland and the great auk, their claim to have named the truly South American penguin is weak. Pennant, writing in 1768, says:

The proper name of these birds is Pinguin (*propter pinguedinem*), on account of their fatness. It has been corrupted to Penguin; so

'The newly-discovered Straits of Magellan. Magellan greets the natives, watched by an enigmatic penguin.' Engraving from *Historiarum Novis Orbis*, by Theodore de Bry, 1620. Courtesy of the Curators of the Bodleian Library

that some, imagining it to have been a Welsh word signifying a white head, entertained some hopes of tracing the British colony, said to have migrated into America, under the auspices of Madoc Gwineth, son of Owen Gwineth, A.D. 1170. But as the two species of birds that frequent that coast have black heads, we must resign every hope founded on that hypothesis of retrieving the Cambrian race in the new world.

Certainly when Sir Francis Drake set sail on his famous circumnavigation from Plymouth on 13 December 1577, he knew all about penguins. (All the more pity that his ship was called *Pelican*.) Until this time British maritime interests had been largely deployed in search of the North West Passage through the Arctic Sea, but now, as relations with Spain grew strained, sea captains like Hawkins and Drake sailed

163

south in search of the trade and plunder that the Spaniards and Portuguese claimed as their exclusive right.

Sir Francis Drake came down the coast of Patagonia and entered the Straits of Magellan in August 1578, where he found 'such plentie of Birds, as is scant credible to report'. On an island named Penguin Island by the early explorers, and subsequently renamed Santa Magdalena, were

> great store of strange birds which could not flie at all, nor yet runne so fast as that they could escape us with their lives; in body they are less than a Goose, and bigger than a Mallard, short and thicke sett together, having no feathers, but instead thereof a certaine hard and matted downe; their beakes are not much unlike the bills of Crowes, they lodge and breed upon the land, where making earthes, as the Conies doe, in the ground, they lay their egges and bring up their young; their feeding and provision to live on is in the sea, where they swimm in such sort, as nature may seeme to have granted them no small prerogative in swiftnesse, both to prey upon others, and themselves, to escape from any others that seeke to seize upon them; and such was the infinite resort of these birds to these Ilands, that in the space of 1 day we killed no lesse than 3000.

These were, of course, magellanic penguins. In 1587, Sir Thomas Cavendish called at this same island and 'powdred three tunnes of Penguins for the victualing of his shippe'. These early southern voyagers regarded the island wildlife as a sort of heaven–sent chandlery store: 'These birds and seals seem to have been bestowed in quantity on those desolate shores, as resources in extremity to distressed voyagers.'

Vessels bound to the East Indies made inroads on the jackass penguins which lived on islands near the Cape of Good Hope. In April 1591, James Lancaster cleared Plymouth in command of three tall ships, the *Penelope*, the *Merchant Royal* and the *Edward Bonaventure*. The fleet was bound for the East Indies, by way of 'the Isles of Comoro and Zanzibar on the backside of Africa'. But although they had luck at the beginning of the voyage, taking a Portuguese caravel laden with wine, '1200 jarres of oyle', olives, capers and other useful necessaries, two men died before they

164

'Resources in extremity to distressed voyagers.' Engraving from *Historiarum Novis Orbis*, by Theodore de Bry, 1620. Courtesy of the Curators of the Bodleian Library

crossed the line, and many others fell ill in these 'wonderful unholesome' latitudes. With the men being 'weake and sicke in all our shippes', they put in to a goodly bay just short of the Cape of Good Hope. Here, badly in need of fresh food, the Admiral took his pinnace to an island 'where he found great store of Penguines and Seales, whereof he brought good plenty with him.' Twice more he sent boats ashore to come back laden.

The hardships of these early voyages of exploration made fearsome reading, but there is no doubt of the quality of the men who undertook them. One of the greatest, a man never properly recognized because he was the victim of unjustified accusations of treachery, was Captain John Davis. Davis had already proved himself a skilful navigator on his journeys in search of the Arctic North-West Passage, when in August 1591 he sailed out of Plymouth in command of the *Desire*, a ship of 140 tons, one of a fleet raised by Sir Thomas Cavendish. With a commission from Queen Elizabeth, Cavendish intended to plunder his way round the world. But all did not go well. Provisioning and supplies were not so

'The known world in 1625.' Title page decoration from *Purchas his Pilgrimes*, by Richard Hakluyt, published posthumously by Samuel Purchas in 1624. Courtesy of the Curators of the Bodleian Library

good as they might have been. One of his ships abandoned the enterprise and returned to England. In a brush with the Portuguese the fleet fared badly. Four remaining vessels finally reached the coast of Patagonia, where they refitted, but during a stormy period in the Magellan Straits, the fleet broke up and scattered. Davis, following his orders, stood on to the east searching for his commander in vain. He never saw him again, but Sir Thomas in a fit of unreasoning injustice accused Davis in his will of 'running away, causing the Decay of the whole Action, and the utter ruin of all'.

John Davis's courage and loyalty were never honoured. Meanwhile, Davis records, on 9 August 1592, 'We had a sore storme, so that we were constrained to hull (heave to), for our sails were not to indure any force.' On the fourteenth, the *Desire* was driven as far west as the Falkland Islands, and thus Davis became the first to discover them. Back he beat to the Magellan Straits.

> The fifth of October our foresayle was split, and all torne; then our Master took the Mizzen, and brought it to the foremast, to make our ship work, and with out sprit-saile we mended our foresayle, the storm continuing without all reason in fury, with haile, snow, rain and wind such and so mighty, as that in nature it could not possibly be more, the seas such and so lofty, with continual breach, that many times we were doubtful whether our ship did sink or swim. We spooned before the sea, three men not being able to guide the helme.

After this, the *Desire* was not seaworthy.

> Our men were not able to move; their sinews were stiff, and their flesh dead, and many of them (which is most lamentably to be reported) were so eaten with lice, as that in their flesh did lie clusters as big as peason, yea and some as big as beans. Being in this miserie we were constrained to put into a cove for the refreshing of our men.

They needed fresh meat and water badly. After yet more disasters, they reached Penguin Island.

> When we came to this Isle we sent out boat on shore, which returned laden with birdes and egges. Our men said that the

Penguins were so thick upon the Isle, that ships might be laden with them; they could not go without treading upon the birds.

Davis sent twenty men ashore to kill and dry penguins, and to take advantage of the respite to regain their health. In time they were 'in as good case as when we came first out of England'. On 22 December 1592, they loaded 14,000 dried penguins into *Desire*. Captain Davis reckoned he needed six months to regain England and he made his calculations accordingly. The daily ration of meat for the crew included five penguins for each four men.

But the journey home was a series of disasters. A shore party collecting fresh water went to sleep unguarded and was attacked and killed by Indians. Davis had to put to sea hurriedly, without the water casks, in order to escape similar treatment. 'Of 76 persons which departed in our ship out of England, we were now left only 27.' They had only enough stinking water with which to wet their lips. The men wanted to give themselves up to the Portuguese, but Davis, who shared every hardship with them, would not allow it.

And now a new disaster struck. The cargo of penguins began to decay in the heat, and the men sickened. Only the penguins were left as provisions, and since they had not been properly dried, they began to breed worms. And the worms multiplied.

> There was nothing they did not devour, only iron excepted. They destroyed shoes, clothing and then they began to eat the ship's timbers, threatening to gnaw through the sides. The more we laboured to kill them, the more they increased. At last we could not sleep for them; they would eat our flesh and bite like mosquitoes.

Yet in spite of loathsome disease and incredible suffering, Davis finally brought *Desire* to the Irish port of Beerhaven in June 1593, sixteen of her crew surviving out of the original seventy-six. He returned to find his name blackened and his achievement unrewarded.

In 1594 Sir Richard Hawkins sailed south in search of trade. He too visited Penguin Island in the Strait of Magellan, and

Some of the many penguin postage stamps

'Of those Fowles they took fifty thousand. Oliver van Noort and ships'
company on Penguin Island.' Engraving from *Historiarum Novis Orbis*,
by Theodore de Bry, 1633. Courtesy of the Curators of the Bodleian
Library

he gives us a description which, despite the fact that it is concerned with the slaughter of the birds, records something more than just the brutal facts.

> The Penguin is in all proportion like unto a Goose, and hath no feathers, but a certaine downe upon all parts of his bodie; and therefore cannot flie, but avayleth himself on all occasions with his feet, running as fast as most men. He liveth in the Sea, and on the Land, feedeth on fish in the Sea, and as a Goose on the shore upon grasse. They harbour themselves under the ground in Burrowes, as the Conies; and in them hatch their young. All parts of the Iland where they haunted were undermined, save only one Valley which (it seemeth) they reserved for their food; for it was as greene as any Medow in the moneth of Aprill, with a most fine short grasse. The flesh of these Pengwins is much of the savour of a certaine Fowle taken in the Ilands of Lundey and Silley, which we call Puffins, by the taste it is easily discerned that they feed on fish. They are very fat, and in dressing must be flead as the Byter; they are reasonable meate rosted, baked, or sodden; but best rosted. We salted some dozen or sixteene Hogsheads, which served us (whilst they lasted) insteed of powdred Beefe.

Astonishing numbers of penguins were sacrificed in order to replenish ship's stores. A few years after Hawkins, Oliver Van Noort came to Penguin Island 'after many tempests. They furnished themselves with store of Penguins and fishes. Of those Fowles they took fifty thousand, being as big as Geese, with egges innumerable, which proved very refreshing to the diseased.'

On those early voyages, with men dying freely from scurvy, desperately in need of fresh food, these penguin islands must have seemed a godsend to hard-pressed Masters. On the first Dutch expedition to the East, Captain William Lodewijckszoon called at a bay near the Cape of Good Hope on 4 August 1595.

> We entered into a haven where we ankered and found good depth at 8 or 9 fadome water, sandy ground. We went on shore to gather fruite, therewith to refresh our sicke men that were thirty or thirty-three in one shippe. In this bay lyeth a small islande wherein are many birdes called Pyncuins that are taken with men's handes.

Not surprisingly, these early mariners were hard put to it to classify these strange animals. Were they bird, beast or fish? Sir Thomas Roe, journeying round southern Africa on his way to present himself as Lord Ambassador to the court of the Great Mogul, cautiously hedges his bets in his journal, making sure not to commit himself irrevocably.

> On Pengwin Island there is a fowle *so called*, that goes upright, his wings without feathers, hanging down like sleeves faced with white: they fly not, but walke in pathes and keep their divisions and quarters orderly; they are a strange fowle, or rather a miscellaneous creature, of Beast, Bird and Fish, but most of Bird, confuting that definition of man to be *Animale bipes implume*, which is nearer to a description of this creature.

Some years later, in 1620, Admiral Beaulieu came to these same islands in his ship *Montmorency*. He too was intrigued by the same jackass penguins, and was sharp enough in his observations, giving us a colourful picture of the island's wildlife.

> We cast anchor within a league of the island, at 20 fathom water, the Ground being muddy Sand. The Isle lay from us North one quarter N.E. and the Southerly waves made us roll prodigiously, so that everything crack'd in the ship. This Island is almost round and about a large League in Circumference. Within, it affords nothing but Sand, and some Bushes, under which the Pinguins hatch their Eggs. A great many rats and Adders live in it, as well as Chameleons and Lizzards. Upon its rocks, but the sea-side, we saw a great many Sea-Bears (seals), which bleat like Sheep, some of which are very large, and have a Skin as thick as a Wolfs, with very soft Hair. Both these and the Pinguins taste very rank of the Oyl of Fish, of which a great quantity might be taken from them, if one were at the pains.
> The Pinguins are Fowls without Wings, which have two Fins, and two broad Paws, upon which they walk upright, and with which they dig the Ground to make their Nests. They are a little bigger than a Cormorant, having a white Belly, a black Back, a very thick Head and a Bill like a Raven's. In the morning they repair to the Sea, where they swim and feed upon Fish, and at night return to their Nests. They have nothing of the taste of Flesh, and for my part, I take them to be feather'd Fish.

'The South African Jackass Penguin.' Note that the bird on the bottom
right has 'a Bill like a Raven's', see page 000. From *A Natural History of
Uncommon Birds*, by George Edwards, 1745

Feathered fish or not, seafarers simply regarded a penguin as a penguin as a penguin, and the realization that there were different species came slowly. Not until 1758 was the first scientific description of a penguin recorded. In that year, in the tenth edition of his *Systema Naturae*, Linnaeus gave the scientific name *Spheniscus demersus* to the South African jackass penguin. And he began the long and confused process of putting order into the muddle of different names, scientific and common, for the different penguins. That same South African penguin, for instance, is known variously in the literature as jackass, black-footed, spectacled or cape penguin, as well as by a handful of different Latin names. In addition to the jackass, sixteen other penguin species were recognized during the next two centuries.

But now, in the middle of the eighteenth century, a new phase of southern seafaring began. England was at peace with the world, the trade routes were established, and the lure of scientific exploration became strong. George the Third inaugurated the first world voyage of scientific exploration. Captain John Byron, RN, commanding the twenty-gun sloop *Dolphin* and the little sixteen-gun *Tamar*, sailed from Plymouth in 1764. He was well equipped. The astrolabe and cross-staff had given place to the reflecting quadrant, forerunner of the present-day sextant; and with the newly-invented ship's chronometer, they could determine longitude within 50km (30 miles). The Royal Observatory at Greenwich provided the most up-to-date tables of declination. Byron, a superb seaman (he was known as Foulweather Jack in the service), was to be one of the first to improve and perfect the charting of the southern seas. *Dolphin* even had her bottom sheathed with copper, a new-fangled and highly successful device to stop the wood-boring teredo 'worm' from eating away the underwater planking.

But although Byron was instructed by the scientists of the Royal Institution, the results of his voyage, splendid as a feat of seamanship, were disappointing. He penetrated no further south than Cape Horn, and made no progress in the charting of the unknown waters below these latitudes. His attitude to

the animals he met depressingly resembled that of the
mariners who had preceded him. When he came to the
Falkland islands, with their teeming seashore world of seals
and sea birds, he records only that his men had to club them
in order to land, so thick were they upon the beach. This was
one of those few occasions, though, when the animals tried to
give back as good as they got. A monster whale charged the
Dolphin, jolting her and splintering her planking. In earlier
days, narwhals had been known to drive their tusks deep into
the sides of a vessel. ('A Sea monster, having a horne, had
therewith stricken against the Ship, with most great strength.
For when we set the Ship on the Strand to make it cleane,
about seven feet under water wee found a Horne sticking in
the Ship, much like for thickness and fashion to a common
Elephant's tooth, not hollow, but full, very strong hard
Bone, which had entered into three Plankes of the Ship, that
is two thicke Planes of Greene, and one of Oken Wood, and
so into a Rib, where it turned upward, to our great good
fortune. It stuck at least halfe a foote deepe into the Ship.')

In 1766 Captain Louis Antoine de Bougainville sailed in *La
Boudeuse* to explore the intricate channels of Tierra del Fuego.
But, in the course of his circumnavigation, he also called at
the Falkland Islands; he gives a sympathetic description of the
king penguin, his interest extending beyond that of most
earlier explorers.

> The penguin of the first class is fond of solitude and retired places.
> It has a peculiar noble and magnificent appearance, having an easy
> gait, a long neck when singing or crying, a longer and more
> elegant bill than the second sort, the back of a more blueish cast,
> the belly of a dazzling white, and a kind of palatine or necklace of
> a bright yellow, which comes down on both sides of the head, as
> a boundary between the blue and the white, and joins on the
> belly. We hoped to be able to bring one of them over to Europe.
> It was easily tamed so far as to follow and know the person that
> had the care of feeding it: flesh, fish and bread, were its food; but
> we perceived that this food was not sufficient and, that it
> absorbed the fatness of the bird; accordingly, when the bird was
> grown lean to a certain degree, it died.

'The penguin of the first class.' Sonnerat's drawing of the king penguin, probably drawn from sketches made by the botanist de Commerçon, who sailed with Louis de Bougainvill. From *Voyage à la Nouvelle Guinée*, by Pierre Sonnerat, 1776

Incidentally, de Bougainville's voyage was the occasion of that first famous circumnavigation by a woman, an adventurous twenty-seven-year-old girl called Baré, who travelled disguised as manservant to the botanist de Commerçon, until she was recognised in due course as female by the canny natives of Tahiti. She was said to have behaved with scrupulous modesty, and eventually returned to St Malo as a heroine. De Bougainville is remembered, of course, for the exotic plant *Bougainvillea*.

A few years after de Bougainville, Lt William Clayton, RN, also visited the Falklands.

I consider the penguins as amphibious animals, partaking of the nature of birds, beasts and fishes. There are four kinds; the yellow, or king penguin; the red; the black or holey, from their burrowing under ground; and the jumping jacks, from their motion. These creatures generally live in the sea, have very short wings which serve for fins, are covered with short thick feathers, and swim at an amazing rate. On shore they walk quite erect with a waddling motion, like a ricketty child; and their breasts and bodies before being quite white, at a distance have, at first sight, the look of a child waddling along with a bib and apron on. They come on shore to lay and hatch their eggs in October: the yolks of the yellow, the holey and jumping penguins, are yellow; but of the red penguins it is red. All their eggs are good nourishing food, and a great refreshment to the seamen; but the flesh of these animals is coarse, fishy, and wholly unfit to eat.

At this time, in the second half of the eighteenth century, no one had yet set foot on the conjectural continent of Antarctica. No European had even seen it. Charts drew vague outlines of a vast continent, *Terra Australis Incognita*, befringed with a sub-Antarctic chain of islands with the chartmaker's symbols ED and PD. Their positions and very existence were indeed doubtful. But in July 1768, Captain James Cook set off on the first of two great voyages, expeditions on which he was to be the first to swing about the world in sub-Antarctic latitudes. A great navigator and the greatest of the explorers, he was the first European, possibly the first man, to come within sighting distance of the

Antarctic mainland coast. One of his officers (on the second voyage), was a German naturalist, John Reinold Forster. Also on the expedition were the scientist and gentleman Joseph Banks, and 'an ingenious and learned Swede', Dr Daniel Carl Solander, a disciple of Linnaeus.

As Cook sailed from Deptford in HMS *Endeavour*, the age of primary discoveries had passed, the age of the scientific explorers was just beginning. Like 'Foulweather Jack' Byron, Cook was sponsored by the Royal Society and laden with the best instruments and charts available; unlike Byron he brought back the goods. His object, achieved in good measure, was to carry out astronomical, geographical and natural science research.

Reading the logs kept by this gallant band of scientists, our penguins at last begin to take shape and life as something more than just a problem for the ship's cook. On 7 January 1769, west of the Falklands, Banks writes:

> Blew strong, yet the ship still Laying too, now for the first time saw some of the birds called Penguins by the Southern navigators; they seem much of the size and not unlike *Alca pica* (Razorbill) but are easily known by streaks upon their faces and their remarkably shrill cry different from any sea bird I am acquainted with.

And on the next day, 'Many Seals and Penguins about the ship, the latter leaping out of the water and diving instantly so that a person unused to them might easily be deceived and take them for fish.' Later, when *Endeavour* was at New Zealand, Banks reported:

> The sea coast is also frequently visited by many Oceanick birds as Albatrosses, Shearwaters, Pintados, &c. and has also a few of the birds called [by Sr. Jno Narborough] Penguins, which are . . . between birds and fishes, as their feathers especially on their wings differ but little from Scales: and their wings themselves, which they use only in diving and by no means in attempting to fly or even accelerate their motion on the surface of the water, might thence almost as properly be called fins.

178

'Lt Clayton's "Red Penguin" (gentoo), from *Voyage à la Nouvelle Guinée*, by Pierre Sonnerat, 1776

'Little Blue Penguin, from New Zealand.' From *A General History of Birds*, by J. Latham, 1824

Cook's first expedition was a success, and on returning to England he refitted without delay and set off a few months later, this time in an ex-Whitby collier, HMS *Resolution* (462 tons), and this time with the object of confirming or disproving the existence of a mid-Pacific continent. But instead of the mythical continent, he made discoveries in the sub-Antarctic. After calling at the Cape of Good Hope, he sailed eastwards down to New Zealand. On 31 March 1773, a shore-party took specimens of little blue penguins from Dusky Bay; these were the first New Zealand penguins to be scientifically described – by Forster, who named them *Eudyptula minor*. At the same time Tobias Furneaux, with *Adventure*, became separated from Cook by a storm, reached Bruni Island, Tasmania, and sheltered in a bay which he named Adventure Bay. He, too, found little blue penguins, but another species as well. And so the first Australian crested penguins were collected.

The expedition now sailed south in search of a southern continent, the much-discussed Terra Australis. On 30 December 1772, in latitude 59° 23′ S, longitude 170° 1′ E, Lt Charles Clerke wrote in his log, 'The meeting with penguins has ever been suppos'd a sign of the vicinity of some land but we've met with so many and are still at a loss for the least bit of Earth.' On the same day, Cook recorded 'Hauled to the Northward for an Island of Ice, thinking if there were any loose pieces about it to take some on board to convert into fresh Water . . . saw upon it about 90 penguins. We fired two 4 pound Shott at them (both missed, TS) . . . but they seemed quite undisturbed.' They pressed on, circling east around the Antarctic Circle, and two years later, running down longitude 110° W, they penetrated through the fog as far south as latitude 71° 10′, the farthest south they ever reached. Solid pack ice and distant icy mountains blocked the way ahead. Cook turned back, correctly believing that the ice, and possibly land, extended as far as the South Pole.

Cook now turned north and then cruised westwards discovering the tropical Pacific islands on his way back to New Zealand. From here, refreshed, the crew of *Resolution* set sail for Cape Horn, running east along latitude 55°. They reached Staten Island, off the tip of Tierra del Fuego, at the end of 1774. Robert Cooper, first lieutenant of *Resolution*, writes laconically in his log for 2 January 1775, 'Today boil'd shags and Penguins in the Coppers for the Ships Company's Dinner.' What did they taste like? On board *Resolution*, sea birds were obviously an important item on the menu. Joseph Gilbert, the master, writes: 'Hoisted in the Launch, having got from the Sea Lyons puncheons of blubber and four boat loads of penguins and shaggs which are exceedingly good eating.' But Lt Clerke commented, 'The people tired of eating penguins and Young Shags, they prefer Salt Beef and Pork to either.'

'Cape Horn.' Woodcut from *A Voyage of Discovery*, by Sir James Clark Ross, 1847

Cook himself was not so keen on eating the 'jumping jackass' penguins at first. 'I cannot say they are good eating, I have indeed made several good meals of them but it was for want of better victuals.' But two weeks later he admitted:

> Got on board a little after 12 o'clock with a quantity of Seals and Penguins, an acceptable present to the Crew . . . any kind of fresh meat was preferred by most on board to Salt; for my own part, I was now, for the first time, heartily tired of salt meat of every kind and prefer'd the Penguins, whose flesh eat nearly as well as bullocks liver, it was however fresh and that was sufficient to make it go down.

John Reinold Forster, the German scientist on *Resolution*, went ashore to describe the magellanic penguins.

> They were of the size of small geese, and of that species which is the most common in the neighbourhood of the Straits of Magelhaens. The English at the Falkland Islands have named them jumping-jacks. They sleep very sound, for Dr Sparrman met one of them, which he kicked several yards by accidentally stumbling over it, without breaking its sleep, till by repeatedly shaking the bird, it awoke. When the whole flock was beset, they all became very bold at once, and ran violently at us, biting our legs, or any part of our clothes. They are excessively hard-lived, for having left a great number of them, seemingly dead on the field of battle, and going in pursuit of the rest, they all at once got up, and walked off with great gravity.

On 17 January 1775, Cook's expedition reached South Georgia, landed and took possession in the name of King George III.

> Here we likewise found a flock of about twenty Penguins, of a much greater size than any we had hitherto seen; they were 39 inches [1m] long, and weighed 40 pounds [18kg]. Their belly was of a most enormous size, and covered with a quantity of fat. An oval spot of bright yellow or lemon-colour appears on each side of the head, and is edged with black, the rest of the body being of a blackish-grey colour on the whole back and upper side, and white on the belly, under the fins, and all the fore part. These birds were so dull as hardly to waddle from us: we easily overtook them by running, and knocked them down with sticks.

'Magellanic Penguin.' From *Voyage à la Nouvelle Guinée*, by Pierre Sonnerat

Forster made a famous drawing of these big king penguins, which he called *Aptenodytes patachonica*, but later the bird was confused with the emperor penguin, which was highly unlikely to be found on South Georgia. The confusion remained for many years, recently to be resolved by one of our present day Antarctic naturalists, Bernard Stonehouse, in the 23rd Scientific Report of the Falkland Islands Dependencies Survey, published in 1960. Forster, who certainly saw the king penguins, but possibly not the emperors, was honoured by Gray in 1844, when he first distinguished between the two species and named the emperor penguin *Aptenodytes forsteri*.

Cook, on a voyage which involved three years, 20,000 leagues, and the most southerly circumnavigation, made Plymouth at the end of July 1775. And the news of his discoveries, and of the unbelievable wealth of animal life in the southern ocean, unleashed fleets of sealing and whaling expeditions to the south. Trade, in the form of ruthless and indiscriminate slaughter, followed the flag with a vengeance. Brave men in small scurvy-ridden ships ravaged the high southern latitudes for the fur seals and sea elephants. By 1791 there were no fewer than 102 vessels engaged in collecting oil and skins in the southern ocean. British sealing expeditions reached South Georgia in 1778, and the Americans were close behind. In less than fifty years they took 1,200,000 fur seals and 20,000 tons of sea-elephant oil reached the London market. In less than a hundred years the South Georgia rookeries had disappeared.

One of the first of the sealers was Captain Edmund Fanning, of the United States. His home port was New York and his ships *Betsey* and *Aspasia*. Fanning was a modest and warmhearted man. He had advanced and considerate views about the treatment of his crew, who seem to have respected him. One of his rules was that he would only sign officers or men who agreed not to swear or to use 'low and vulgar language'. Nothing was lost by this rule he says, and 'a prominent part of our agreement was that all the quarrelling and swearing on board was to be done by myself, and the

185

work by them. This has ever readily been agreed to, nor could I ever discover any advantage in governing seamen by coarse oaths.'

Fanning was looking for fur seals, but when he reached the Falkland Islands he took time off to visit the penguins.

After sending on board the ship some geese and ducks which we had shot soon after landing, we started, taking along a large salt basket in which to bring back some eggs for supper; for the bird rookery, which lies up a valley, on the opposite or sea-board side of the island, is at a distance of something like three-quarters of a mile across to it. This rookery (as it is called) contains, or extends over, a patch of ground of from four to six acres, on a side hill, surrounded with high bogs of the coarse grass called tussucks. Over this area, the birds, such as the albatrosses, penguins, and shags, have their nests, and to all appearance cover the entire surface in one grand assemblage. In fact so closely side by side are they mixed together, that there is considerable difficulty in walking among them, great caution being necessarily exercised lest one should tread upon them, for they are so void of fear as to suffer themselves to be taken with the hand; yet in order to proceed, one is constantly obliged to push and kick them out of the way. On their part nothing backward, they return this rough

Captain Edmund Fanning's ASPASIA

manner of proceeding, with a continual pecking and biting at the hands and feet, frequently with such a painful nip as to start the blood. A continued cackling is kept up by this feathered fraternity to such a degree of clamourousness, that persons walking among them, within a yard of each other, cannot understand what their companions are speaking about, or even hear them, unless the speaker calls out in a loud voice what he has to say.

There are four different kinds of the amphibious bird, viz. the King penguin, which is the largest, the Jackass penguin, the John penguin and the Mackaronie: it is this last only, that inhabits the rookeries with the albatrosses; the other three keeping by themselves.

The Mackaronie is about sixteen inches [40cm] high, and has on each side of its head a tuft of thin feathers, richly variegated in color, which gives the bird a very consequential and proud appearance. In its walk, or rather march, it is as erect as a soldier. One could sit for hours, and observe their manner of approaching the shore, after a spell of feeding in the sea; to effect this purpose, they make choice of a spot where the sea breaks directly against the side of the rocks, and while yet some seventy yards from the landing place, swimming moderately along in solid columns of hundreds together, toward it, commence diving and coming up again to the surface at short distances; this is continued until about within thirty feet of their landing, when they dive again, and come up in the surf ten or twelve feet from the rock, with such velocity as to land upon it perfectly erect, and clear of the surf; immediately forming an Indian file, and divided into distinct bodies, each division having its own leader, whom they follow, proceeding in their march up the valley or chasm, to the rookery, apparently with as much conceit of their superiority in point of discipline as ever a company of soldiers manifested on a public parade. The gratification derived from beholding a scene like this, is in a great measure counterbalanced, in the destruction committed among them by the sea-lions, which place themselves a few rods from the landing place, in the water, watching the time that the penguins are about to commence diving to land, at which period they are the most compact. At this moment, the lion settles himself under water with the intention of swimming under them, and when a suitable opportunity offers, rises suddenly in their midst, and seizes one or more of the birds in his jaws; then raising part of his ponderous body out of the water, he

'King Penguin.' From *Philosophical Transactions*, by Thomas Pennant, 17

bites and shakes this, his prey, until they are torn in pieces, then devouring them. It frequently happens that some of these birds get badly wounded in the legs or wings, and land in this maimed condition; whenever this is the case, they are instantly attacked by their comrades, who peck and bite them until they rise up and take their places in the line of march, or until, by this tormenting, they are killed.

Captain Fanning subsequently visited South Georgia on probably the most profitable sealing voyage ever made there, when he collected the astonishing number of 57,000 fur-seal skins. He took them to China for sale, getting five to six dollars apiece. At the same time, sixteen other American and British vessels were working at South Georgia.

In 1810 an Australian sealing expedition discovered Macquarie Island, with its vast rookeries of royal penguins, later to be the cause of a highly-profitable oil industry. But at first the interest of the Australians was in the fur-seal herds, and six vessels engaged in the task of decimating them. The slaughter on the islands of the southern ocean was so intense, and so ignorantly conducted, that it could hardly last for many years. When the Russian explorer Bellingshausen, with the ships *Vostok* and *Mirnyi*, reached the high southern latitudes in 1820, he found that the fur seals were already extinct on Macquarie Island, and that those on South Georgia were rapidly following the same path.

In the South Shetlands he found British and American sailing ships carving up what was left of the fur seals and sea elephants. One captain told Bellingshausen that he had taken 60,000 seals in one season. The sealers were slaughtering penguins in thousands, using their tough skins as fuel for melting the blubber. In the South Shetlands alone, 320,000 fur seals were killed in 1821 and 1822. Only the adults were taken and more than 100,000 pups were left to die. Not surprisingly, the species was nearly exterminated in the islands. In the next fifty years the survivors had time to recover and build up stocks, only to have the whole process of slaughter begin again. On the other islands the same dismal story was repeated.

In the long run the only factor that saved these magnificent sea creatures was that there came a point, on each island, when the seal populations were too low to present an economical proposition to the hunter. On all the accessible beaches, pitiful numbers of survivors remained to form the nucleus of a new rookery.

Three hundred years after Magellan, Captain Fitz Roy, RN, brought the barque *Beagle* to the Falklands, on the way to Tierra del Fuego and the Strait of Magellan for a surveying voyage. On board was a twenty-two-year-old naturalist, Charles Darwin. In his log, dated March 1834, Darwin writes:

Another day, having placed myself between a penguin (Aptenodytes demersa) and the water, I was much amused by watching its habits. It was a brave bird; and till reaching the sea, it

'Seal Hunting.' Sketched by Joseph Hooker, assistant surgeon on HMS *Erebus*, with Sir James Clark Ross. From *A Voyage of Discovery*, by Sir James Clark Ross, 1847

'Tussac Grass of Falkland Islands.' From *A Voyage of Discovery*, by Sir James Clark Ross, 1847

regularly fought and drove me backwards. Nothing less than heavy blows would have stopped him: every inch he gained he firmly kept, standing close before me erect and determined. When thus opposed he continually rolled his head from side to side, in a very odd manner, as if the power of distinct vision lay only in the anterior and basal part of each eye. This bird is commonly called the jackass [now Magellanic] from its habit, while on shore, of throwing its head backwards, and making a loud strange noise, very like the braying of an ass; but while at sea, and undisturbed, its note is very deep and solemn, and is often heard in the night-time. In diving its little wings are used as fins; but on the land, as front legs. When crawling, it may be said on four legs, through the tussocks or on the side of a grassy cliff, it moves so very quickly that it might easily be mistaken for a quadruped. When at sea and fishing, it comes to the surface for the purpose of breathing with such a spring, and dives again so instantaneously, that I defy any one at first sight to be sure that it was not a fish leaping for sport.

191

In 1839 an expedition under the command of Dumont d'Urville, in *Astrolabe*, visited the South Orkneys and the South Shetlands, pushing deeper south to discover the Antarctic Adélie Land, where he took possession for France. He also took possession of specimens of the penguins he found, and to these birds he also gave the name Adélie, after his wife. During the course of his voyage he retrieved from an ice floe an egg which later proved to belong to an emperor penguin. But the formal scientific discovery of this, the greatest of all the penguins, was denied him. In that same year, a British expedition, under Admiralty instructions and the command of Captain James Clark Ross, set off to make a series of magnetic observations in high southern latitudes for the British Association for the Advancement of Science. Ross, with HMS *Erebus* and HMS *Terror*, reached Hobart, Tasmania, in August 1840, to hear of Dumont d'Urville's successes.

'Impressed with the feeling that England had ever *led* the way of discovery', Ross determined to penetrate deeper south if possible. Obstructed by land he followed the coast of Antarctica till he was able to turn south down the 170° E meridian, where he discovered what we now call the Ross Sea. In the beginning of January 1842, in latitude 66° S and longitude 156° W, *Erebus* and *Terror* were drifting with the pack ice, searching for the lead which would eventually reveal their great discoveries. On the ice floes were parties of emperor penguins. These birds must of course have been seen by earlier voyagers, but now they were collected and positively identified for the first time. Ross's published account of the voyage records that:

> During the last few days we saw many of the great penguins, and several of them were caught and brought on board alive. These enormous birds varied in weight from sixty to seventy-five pounds [27–34kg]. The largest was killed by the *Terror*'s people, and weighed seventy-eight pounds [35kg]. They are remarkably stupid and allow you to approach them so near as to strike them on the head with a bludgeon, and sometimes, if knocked off the ice into the water, they will almost immediately leap upon it

192

again as if to attack you, but without the smallest means either of offence or defence.

Some of these were preserved entire in casks of strong pickle, that the physiologist and comparative anatomist might have an opportunity of thoroughly examining the structure of this wonderful creature. Its principal food consists of various species of cancri and other crustaceous animals; and in its stomach we frequently found from two to ten pounds' [1–4·5kg] weight of pebbles, consisting of granite, quartz, and trappean rocks. Its capture afforded great amusement to our people, for when alarmed and endeavouring to escape, it makes its way over deep

'HMS *Erebus* and *Terror* pushing through the pack ice. Emperor Penguin in foreground.' From *A Voyage of Discovery*, by Sir James Clark Ross, 1847

snow faster than they could follow it: by lying down on its belly and impelling itself by its powerful feet, it slides along upon the surface of the snow at a great pace, steadying itself by extending its fin-like wings which alternately touch the ground on the side opposite to the propelling leg. . . . I was in the habit of examining the stomachs of most of the birds which I shot and preserved for the Government Collection; and found the penguins my best geological collectors, for their crops were frequently filled with pebbles; more especially the large species, *Aptenodytes antarctica.* In one of these individuals I found upwards of a pound of small fragments of rocks; comprising, basalt, greenstone, porphyry, granite, vesicular lava, quartz, scoriae, and pumice.

By this time land had been sighted at points all around the coast of Antarctica. With the emperor, the only other truly Antarctic penguin species, the adélie, had been made known to science. The Patagonian, the sub-Antarctic island, the South African and the antipodean species had almost all been described. One writer was rash enough to say that there were no more penguins to be found. But in 1871 the only

'Catching the Emperor Penguins.' From *A Voyage of Discovery*, by Sir James Clark Ross, 1847

'The discovery of Possession Island, Victoria Land', 14 January 1841.
From *A Voyage of Discovery*, by Sir James Clark Ross, 1847

equitorial penguin, *Spheniscus mendiculus*, was 'discovered',
established in the Galapagos Islands, 970km (600 miles) west
of Ecuador. In 1874 the white-flippered penguin, a sub-
species of the little blue, was found on the Banks Peninsula of
the South Island of New Zealand. The royal penguin of
Macquarie Island, although well known to the early sealers,
was not made known scientifically till 1876. Such was the
confusion over penguin names that in one case, that of the
snares island penguin, the species was not recognized till
1953.

Penguins, as individuals, have had to endure gross treatment. The attitude of the discoverers was often one of simple
greed and the unfortunate penguin regarded only as a tasty,
or untasty, meal. But perhaps it would be idle to deny that
any of us would regard them otherwise, after several months
of anxious and highly uncomfortable voyaging in

195

'Woolly Penguin'. From *A General History of Birds*,
by J. Latham, 1824

uncharted waters in cramped ships, living on weevily biscuits and salt beef. But if we are tempted ever to feel complacent about our present-day attitude to penguins – there's no doubt it is vastly more enlightened and that international conservation of Antarctic wildlife is a strong possibility – then we have only to read a passage from the journal of one of our own contemporaries, Eric Hiscock (*Around the World in Wanderer III*, Oxford University Press, 1956). Eric Hiscock is a fine seaman who, in the course of his first circumnavigation of the world, followed the wake of Captain Cook's voyage of 180 years earlier, when he cruised the coasts of Australia. On a cheerless, drizzly evening, Hiscock was taken by friends to see the 'evening parade' of a colony of little penguins on Philipp Island. 'A grey angry-looking sea was breaking heavily on the sand beach. The day being a Sunday there were about 150 people waiting there to watch the evening miracle, most of them, like ourselves, huddling in the lee of the sandhills. The rookery is a honeycomb of holes scooped out of the sand dunes well above reach of the sea and there the hen lays her two, or occasionally three, eggs. During the breeding season, which lasts from mid-October to the end of March, the cock penguins leave the rookery at dawn to spend the day fishing. At dusk, heavily laden with the day's catch, they all return to Surf Bay, where they land on one small section only of the long beach exactly opposite the rookery and waddle up to their homes, where they disgorge the fish for the benefit of hens and chicks.

'As I sat that evening looking at the heavy swell in the fading light, I could not help but wonder whether we were going to see this much talked-of miracle. For one thing I did not understand how a bird which is incapable of flying could ever find its way back to the home beach after swimming many miles offshore, for with a height of eye of only an inch or two it would be incapable of seeing the land unless it was very close. Even, I argued, supposing the penguin could navigate so accurately by some sixth sense of which we know nothing, it would surely be physically impossible for any bird to make a landing through the surf which was running on the beach that evening. But then as I looked around at the huddled figures waiting expectantly, I felt that surely something remarkable was going to happen and I grew increasingly excited.

'And suddenly the amazing thing did happen. A roller broke on the beach, and as its backwash went sucking down the sand to meet the next one coming in, I saw a small dark head and stout beak appear above the white, lacy, foam. Then to left and right another and another head popped above the surface of the water and soon thirty or forty little penguins with blue-grey heads and backs and snow-white breasts were struggling to get a foothold. But before they managed to reach the shore the next breaker burst over them, hiding them from my sight. I felt desperately sorry for them, for they would be heavily laden and tired after the day's long swim, but there was nothing I could do to help. When, however, that breaker receded I was thankful to see that the birds were a little closer than before, and eventually, having been overwhelmed by yet another breaker, they reached the beach, to my great relief. One of their number then advanced and with outstretched wings marshalled the party into a compact formation, and when he was satisfied he went ahead leading the way up the beach. All this was, unfortunately, too much for some of the onlookers who got to their feet and ran about excitedly in front of the birds, shining torches on them and taking flashlight photographs. The bright lights must temporarily have blinded the penguins, whose eyes are accustomed to the dim green light of the sea and the twilight of the burrows. For a moment they stopped, bewildered; then the leader turned, raised his wings and herded the entire party back into the cold, grey and unfriendly sea from which they had only just made their way with such difficulty. Frank and I, shocked and sickened at such behaviour, shouted at the hooligans to stay still and leave the birds alone. This had some effect, for the next time the party made a landing it was left almost undisturbed to struggle, with bodies leaning slightly forward, up the beach

198

to the rookery. From that time on and at irregular intervals more and more penguins arrived, probably a total of between four and five hundred; but on several occasions the antics of the onlookers frightened some of them back into the sea. It was dark by the time the final landing was made, and by then all the other onlookers had gone. So we were able to watch the last platoon plodding undisturbed up the beach close by us.'

7 · Exploitation

Penguins are exploited for their meat, their blubber and their skins. Their eggs are marketed in quantities and even their droppings harvested as guano. They are easy prey because of their inability to fly and their relative lack of fear. Since their main enemies are in the sea, their escape response is to flee on to land and into the metaphorical arms of their captors. They are gregarious, crowding together readily and conveniently.

Before Europeans came on the scene, South American Indians like the Alacaluf and Yahgan tribes already raided the penguin colonies by canoe. Apart from the meat, they used the skins for decorative purposes; the Yahgans made purses of penguin skin, for instance. Disappointingly, there is no record of penguin motifs appearing on pre-Columbian pottery, although other birds such as harpy eagles and andean condors were common enough. In New Zealand the Maoris are known to have taken albatrosses and sooty petrels, and it seems reasonable to assume they also took penguins. They preserved young birds in fat, a delicacy known as *hua hua*, in flaxen bags protected by an outer layer of bark.

EGGS

All penguin eggs are edible, and possibly more important than the flesh as a source of food. They tend to have red yolks, presumably on account of the carotenoid pigment in the birds' crustacean food. The sealers stored quantities of eggs between layers of sand after immersing them in seal oil. On one raid alone, a rockhopper colony was relieved of fifty-six barrels of eggs. In 1832 one ship's crew collected fifty barrels of magellan eggs at Cabo dos Bahias. They used an egg hook consisting of an iron hoop on the end of a pole to extract the egg from deep in the nest burrow.

In South Africa, Malays and other coloured men sold the large greenish eggs of the jackass penguin in the markets of Cape Town. In 1896 they were fetching 2s a dozen, and the annual harvest of eggs from Dassen Island alone was something of the order of 300,000; the colonial government enjoyed a revenue amounting to about £700 a year from this source. Dassen Island lies some 60km (40 miles) north of Cape Town, about 10km (6 miles) from the mainland. It is a flat island, hardly rising more than 6 or 9m (20 or 30ft) above sea level, 3km (2 miles) by 1·5km (1 mile) in extent. Everywhere the ground is riddled with burrows 30cm (1ft) or so in depth, each burrow the home of a pair of penguins. Philip Sclater, who saw the egg harvest in action, says it was impossible to look in any direction without seeing countless numbers of penguins. The egging season, 15 February to 15 August, was worked by men who marched in a long line across the island in different directions every day, each man armed with a basket and a kitchen ladle tied to the end of a long stick, used for scooping the eggs from underneath the birds.

On Tristan da Cunha, rockhopper eggs are an important source of food. Early in this century as many as 25,000 a year were taken (on one particular day 7,200), but by 1938 the toll was reduced to 10–12,000 a year.

In the Falkland Islands egg-collecting was a traditional affair reaching the status of social ritual. On Lord Mayor's

Day, 9 November, the islanders had an egging picnic. One of these forays resulted in 13,000 eggs being removed from a two-kilometre (one mile) stretch of cliff. Since the collector runs the risk of being smothered in jackass fleas, the Lord Mayor presumably delegated one of his minions to act as his representative. For the children the spree was lengthened into 'egging week', and some of the rockhopper colonies near the Falkland capital, Stanley, could not take the strain and eventually disappeared. An average consumption of eggs in the Falklands is said to have been sixty-one per year per person.

Gentoo eggs are said to be the favourite, and a rough estimate is that nowadays 10,000 a year may be harvested, under government licence. However there is not much doubt that a certain amount of unofficial collecting is done on the side; certainly there are fewer eggs for the taking. In 1911, 85,000 eggs were collected from the Kidney Islands, while in 1952 the result of an exhaustive search was 1,000.

On South Georgia the penguin colonies were always fair game for the sealers, but indiscriminate and senseless egging continued well into the twentieth century. The American scientist Robert Cushman Murphy visited the island in 1912, on board the sealing brig *Daisy*. His work was severely hampered by the ignorance and stupidity of the crew. The sailors and officers freely raided the penguins, and in one case removed every egg from two whole rookeries of the already hard-pressed kings. Many of the eggs contained large embryos and since they could be neither eaten nor blown, were thrown overboard. As a result of this vandalism, Murphy saw no young kings during his visit.

SKINS

Penguins have such fine, dense feathers, evenly distributed over their bodies, that the skins have been put to a number of uses in the world of fashion. The Indians of Tierra del Fuego made good use of penguins 'whose Flesh yeelded them food, their Skinnes clothing' and made themselves 'a Cloke of

Penguin skinnes' according to Hakluyt, who also says: 'These skinnes they compact together with no less industrie and Art than Skinners do with us.'

In the last twenty-five years of the nineteenth century there was a thriving market in magellanic penguin skins in Montevideo and Buenos Aires, where the white feathered parts were used for trimming women's clothes. Peruvian penguin skins were used to make 'fur' caps and purses. The Antarctic explorers and, in our own day, the Antarctic scientists, used king penguin skins to prepare fancy slippers.

On Tristan da Cunha penguin skins have always had commercial value. The islanders kill rockhoppers in April after the moult in order to get the trapeze-shaped head skin with its projecting golden plumes. Each skin is scraped of blubber and hung out to dry; then perhaps as many as thirty skins are sewn together to make the highly prized tassel mats. More recently the islanders have begun to make caps modelled on those worn by American sailors. They also make purses and bags from the skins. All these articles serve as a much-needed source of income, when bartered for goods and money.

When the penguins are moulting, they are rounded into pens like sheep, and the loose masses of feathers stripped off. These are used for mattresses – no doubt after the fleas have been dealt with.

Magellanic Penguin

Oil

The thick layer of fat beneath penguin skins, 2cm (¾in) thick in the case of kings, has been eagerly exploited. In 1867 one company is reported to have collected 50,700 gallons (230,500 litres) of blubber from 405,600 birds. At 1s 7½d (8p) a gallon this fetched £4,119, a formidable sum at that time. It was this kind of slaughter which eventually roused naturalists to press for legislation.

On Tristan da Cunha the penguins were allocated on a family basis, each family taking eighty rockhoppers during the month of March. Each rockhopper yielded half a litre (one pint) of oil, which was used mainly for lighting.

King penguins on South Georgia were boiled in large quantities for oil by traders. Klutschak, who visited the island in 1877 aboard an American schooner, wrote:

> Human greed has been the cause of great persecution of these creatures. I am told (although personally I cannot vouch for it) that oil made from penguin fat was formerly utilized in tanning leather, and that vessels came for the purpose of taking these birds in huge numbers in order to extract the oil. This commodity, which must always have been expensive, has now been superseded by cheaper and perhaps better chemical preparations, hence the destruction of the penguins has ceased. Proof that they were slaughtered in former times, however, may be seen along the whole northern and northeastern coasts where the small iron trypots, always arranged in pairs, still lie about. At French Harbour parts of a French penguin-hunting ship, which was wrecked in this labyrinth of reefs, may still be seen.

But the most famous of all penguin-oil factories was on the Macquarie Islands. In 1891 Joseph Hatch was granted a lease by the New Zealand government to collect penguin oil. The episode lasted more than twenty-five years, was highly successful, but finally succumbed in the face of organized public opposition.

Royal Penguin

At first, Hatch concentrated on the king penguins but found that it was difficult to extract their oil without getting it contaminated with blood, so he turned his attention to the smaller but much more plentiful royal penguins. The season began in February, when the year-old juveniles, or 'fats', came ashore to moult. Later, in March, the adult birds were taken, the season lasting six weeks, in which time something like 150,000 birds were dealt with. But in spite of these numbers, and probably by accident, the arrangement involved the least possible damage to the population, taking place before the breeding season began, and involving only a fraction of the incoming birds. So long as the number taken in a season did not exceed the potential annual increase, the system could, and almost did, continue indefinitely.

The birds were herded into pens, killed and placed in the 'digesters', 900 representing a 'charge'. The dead birds were carried to the upper part of the digester along a railed plank. And it was this part of the process which gave rise to the totally false story of penguins being driven *alive* up a ramp until they fell into the boiling vat. Each bird yielded half a litre (one pint) of oil and it fetched £18 per ton.

Joseph Hatch was vilified on all sides. The 'boiling alive' story, widely believed, had the general public and scientific societies howling for *his* blood. He survived a great deal of organized opposition and litigation, but the final straw to the public came when he claimed that there were more royal penguins on Macquarie than when he had begun operations. No one would swallow this, Hatch was branded a liar as well as a rogue, and the government was finally persuaded to terminate his lease. Scientists have since studied all the available data and come to the conclusion that Joseph Hatch was telling the truth, and that in fact the rookery was expanding in size during the period of his depredations.

Guano

Guano is an Inca word for the naturally dessicated dung of fish-eating sea fowl. The Peruvian deposits date back to 500 BC, although new dating techniques may well prove them to have started much earlier. Certainly prehistoric farmers used the nitrogen-rich guano to improve their crops. The Incas protected the birds and extracted the guano on a sensible basis, taking it at a rate slower than it was produced. Later harvesters were not so enlightened, and set about killing the golden goose with the usual enthusiasm.

From the early nineteenth century guano was a major product of international trade. Between 1848 and 1875 more than 20,000,000 tons were shipped to Europe and the United States. In the early twentieth century the deposits began to fail and Peruvian agriculture became seriously short of fertilizer. From 1909 a more sensible policy was pursued and the guano treated as a crop instead of a limitless resource. The sea-bird islands became sanctuaries, with walled defences against pests, and the situation stabilized and improved. Now

Peruvian Booby

a new danger threatens, as the possibility of large-scale harvesting of plankton endangers the sea-birds' hunting grounds.

The chief guano-producing birds are cormorants, boobies, pelicans and penguins – in South America the peruvian penguin and in South Africa the jackass.

In 1983, 6,406 tons of guano were collected from the islands of South and South-west Africa, valued at 1,300,000 rand. Along with the many thousands of penguin eggs, it provides a useful resource, but unfortunately it is very expensive to collect the guano and administer and maintain the system! But because the manure is so valuable to the market gardener the government subsidizes the operation.

PROTECTION

Legal protection for penguins was non-existent until the nineteenth century, and not until the early 1900s was it begun in earnest. In 1905 the International Ornithological Congress in London passed a resolution urging the governments of Australia and New Zealand to put an end to the destruction of penguins, which were being boiled for their oil. South Georgia penguins were protected from 1909. In the Falkland Islands, where penguins had enjoyed a measure of protection since 1864, all penguins were protected by 1914. In 1919, the Tasmanian government stopped all licences to exploit penguins on Macquarie Island and it was proclaimed a sanctuary.

In 1924 the French declared the Kerguelen Islands a National Park. But it was 1959 before a major conference of nations, twelve altogether, signed the Antarctic Treaty, agreeing on the need to protect Antarctica from despoilment and to conserve its living resources. Eventually it is hoped that Antarctica will become an international wildlife reserve, and that all penguins everywhere will get the protection they have so dearly earned.

8 · Species Notes

SOUTH AFRICA

14

PRINCE EDWARD Is.
2.4.9

∴ CROZET Is.
2.4.9

TRISTAN da CUNHA ・ 8 ・ GOUGH Is. 8

BOUVET Is. 5.9

2.4.8.9.
KERGUELEN Is. 1

HEARD Is. ・
2.4.5.9

SOUTH SANDWICH
2.5.9.

SOUTH GEORGIA
2.4.5.9.

ANTARCTICA
1,2,3,4,5,8.

4.5.9.8.
S. ORKNEYS

4.5.9.8.
S. SHETLANDS

FALKLAND Is.
4.8.9.16.

16.

STATEN Is.
2.4.16.

8

SOUTH AMERICA

16.

・ PETER Is
4

・ BALLE
4

15.

CAMPBELL
7, 8, 10, 12

・ JUAN FERNANDEZ
15

7.8 ANTIPODES Is.
7.8 BOUNTY Is.

13. CHATHAM

・ GALAPAGOS 17

The distribution and main breeding areas of Penguins.

1 Emperor

2 King

3 Adélie

4 Gentoo

5 Chinstrap

6 Fiordland Crested

7 Erect Crested

8 Rockhopper

9 Macaroni

10 Royal

11 Snares Island

12 Yellow-eyed

13 Little

14 Jackass

15 Peruvian

16 Magellanic

17 Galápagos

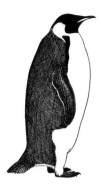

EMPEROR PENGUIN *Aptenodytes forsteri* (Gray)
Spanish: Pinguin Emperador

Length 120cm (4ft). Long, rather slender and decurved bill, patches of orange-yellow at sides of neck. Weighs from 23 to 45kg (50 to 100lb). One of the world's largest and heaviest sea birds. Although substantially heavier than the king penguin, it has relatively smaller wings, feet and bill, factors favouring heat retention.

Breeds only on the continent of Antarctica, assembling on the sea ice below ice cliffs. The most truly Antarctic of all birds. No nest. After the egg is laid, soon after the sea ice forms in autumn, the male takes charge of it, carrying it on top of the feet, warmed by a fold of skin on his belly. While the male fasts, the female travels, perhaps many miles, across the sea ice in order to reach open water and feed. Towards the end of the sixty-day incubation period she returns to relieve the male and feed the chick. The males then disperse after the long fast. The young are reared during the winter months achieving independence during the short summer season when food is abundant. In October and November, at the beginning of the Antarctic summer, they begin an extraordinary migration, congregating in groups at the edge of the sea ice, waiting for the ice to break and provide ice-floe rafts on which they drift northward. The survival of the juvenile depends on their ice floe lasting long enough to allow them to complete their moult before they have to enter the water.

Emperors normally walk bolt upright, but if alarmed they drop down and 'toboggan', using wings and legs to propel themselves. Main predators are sea leopards and killer whales.

210

KING PENGUIN *Aptenodytes patagonicus* (Miller)
Spanish: Pinguin Real

Length 90cm (3ft). Weighs 14 to 18kg (30 to 40lb). Similar in appearance to emperor penguin, but differs in size and in having brighter yellow colouration.

Breeds in the Antarctic and sub-Antarctic islands (being replaced on Polar coasts by the emperor), on Prince Edward, Crozet, Kerguelen, Heard, Macquarie, South Georgia, South Sandwich and Staten Islands. Wanders north to Tierra del Fuego and the Falklands. Rookeries are always on low, bare ground, where the birds incubate the single egg in a fashion similar to that of the emperor. Incubation period is about fifty-four days, both parents sharing. Kings are more or less sedentary; their shore-territory is never completely choked with ice, and their food, squid and sprats, is close at hand in the inshore kelp-beds.

At sea, the main predator is the leopard seal. On shore, man has wrought enormous damage over the years, many hundreds of thousands of birds having been taken for their plumage and their blubber, with the result that the range of the species is much reduced, although its numbers are now increasing.

ADÉLIE PENGUIN *Pygoscelis adeliae* (Hombron and Jacquinot)
or Black-throated Penguin
Spanish: Pinguin de Adelia

Length about 75cm (30in). The most familiar of all penguins, the smart little man in evening dress. Weight about 4–6kg (9–14lb) dropping to 3–5kg (6–10lb) after the breeding season.

Antarctic and circumpolar. Most abundant and widely distributed of all Antarctic penguins. Vagrant to South Georgia, Heard Island and Macquarie Island. Does not breed north of the South Sandwich and Bouvet Islands.

Adélies return to the rookery during October, when the sea is still frozen and they may have to cross as much as

100km (60 miles) of ice. They nest at the foot of gentle ice-cliff slopes. Experienced breeders return to the same nest site and construct a nest-pile of small stones (no other material is available) on open ground. Two eggs (sometimes only one but never three), incubated at first by male while female goes off to feed at sea (mainly on shrimps), returning to relieve her mate two weeks later. Subsequently they take turns in departing for feeding expeditions. Incubation period is about thirty-six days. Both parents feed the young, which after four weeks congregate in crèches of as many as a hundred or more chicks. Returning parents recognize and feed their own chicks in the group. Juveniles moult, then go to sea in February. Walking speed about 5km (3 miles) an hour, but adélies can run or toboggan much faster, outdistancing a sprinting man.

Predators at the rookery are sheathbills and antarctic skuas, but the weather is a more important enemy, many birds being buried at their nests by snow blizzards. At sea the main predator is the leopard seal.

GENTOO PENGUIN *Pygoscelis papua* (Forster)
or Johnny Penguin. Sometimes Rockhopper *or* Jackass, but in confusion with other species
Spanish: Pinguin de Pico Rojo, Juanito

Length 75cm (30in). Only penguin with conspicuous white marks on top of head. White band extends from eye to eye across a slaty black head. Bluish-black back. Bill yellowish-orange. Feet orange-yellow with black claws. Unaggressive. Weight 4–5.8kg (9–13lb).

Circumpolar in Antarctic and sub-Antarctic zones, breeding on Graham Land, Falkland Islands, South Orkneys, South Shetlands, Staten Island, South Georgia, Macquarie, Prince Edward, Marion, Crozet, Kerguelen and Heard Islands.

Rookeries are on mounds amongst the tussock grass or on low hill-tops. Two eggs (first favourite of the sealers) laid in

September/October. Nest of grass, leaves, twigs or pebbles (even pieces of tin or shotgun-cartridge cases). Both parents incubate, for about thirty-three days. Young fed on shrimp and squid by regurgitation. Subsquently form crèches.

The adults normally walk in a deliberate manner, following well-trodden paths between sea and nest-site, but toboggan if pressed. Prefer to enter sea from a shelving beach rather than jump from a ledge. Fast swimmers. Predators on land, skuas; at sea, leopard seals.

CHINSTRAP PENGUIN *Pygoscelis antarctica* (Forster)
or Ringed Penguin, Bearded Penguin, Stonecracker
Spanish: Pinguin de Collar, Pinguin de Barbijo

Length 75cm (30in). Similar in appearance to the adélie, except for a distinguishing narrow black line (the chinstrap) which crosses the throat to join the black of the back of the head. Weight about 4kg (9lb).

Abundant, but restricted in distribution: North Graham Land, South Shetlands, South Orkneys, South Sandwich and east to Bouvet Islands. Small numbers on South Georgia, Peter First and Heard Islands. Vagrant to Falklands.

Pugnacious character. Ear-splitting voice. Comes to the breeding places with the Antarctic spring. Two eggs, laid in a simple nest-scoop rimmed with a few pebbles, normally on bare terrain. Pairs crowded off the main colony may build on snow, which subsequently melts, leaving the sitting bird at the bottom of a hole. Chinstraps hatch later than adélies and gentoos, but their rate of growth is faster. The juveniles do not form crèches, but remain within the family territory.

Walks on ice or hard ground, propels itself when tobogganing with its feet only, climbs on all fours. Less inclined to progress on its belly. When in haste its flippers perform a 'rowing' action, instead of moving alternatively. Feeds on crustaceans and small fish.

Predators: skua in the rookery, leopard seal in the sea.

213

FIORDLAND CRESTED PENGUIN *Eudyptes pachyrhynchus* (Gray)
or Thick-billed Penguin
Maori: Tauake

(Most of the penguins in the *Eudyptes* genus are found in the New Zealand area. Birds of medium size with stout bills and long tail, they have yellow superciliary crests on sides of head. Blue above and white below with a dark throat.)

Length 50–70cm (20–28in). Bill shorter and more elevated, crest commencing at nostrils and not extending much behind eye.

Sub-Antarctic islands and mainland of New Zealand. Spends the winter at sea, coming ashore in July.

No nest is built; the two pale-green eggs are laid in July, in caves or in deep cavities beneath tree-roots in coastal forest. Incubation period about six weeks. Nocturnal on land. Probably frequents caves and secluded places in order to escape the unwelcome attentions of sandflies.

Feeds on small fish, crustaceans and cuttlefish. Chicks remain in nest cave as much as seven months and reach full adult plumage at twelve months.

ERECT-CRESTED PENGUIN *Eudyptes sclateri* (Buller)
or Sclater's Penguin, Auckland Islands Penguin, Big-crested Penguin

Length 70cm (28in). The only crested penguin with an erect crest: no part of the crest comes below the bird's eye level.

Australian and New Zealand seas, breeding in large numbers mainly at Bounty and Antipodes Islands, smaller numbers at Campbell and Auckland Islands.

Two pale-blue eggs laid in a muddy hollow among rocks or ledges close to high-water mark. One of the eggs almost invariably gets kicked out of the nest and only one is incubated. The chatter of these penguins in their dense rookeries is said to be deafening and the stench almost unbearable. At suitable landing places there is a constant stream of dirty penguins taking headers into the sea and incoming clean birds diving a few yards offshore then shooting up on a wave and clinging to the rocks with bill, flippers and feet.

ROCKHOPPER PENGUIN *Eudyptes chrysocome* (Miller) *or* Victoria Penguin, Crested Penguin, Jumping Jackass, Redfooted Penguin (Pennant)
Spanish: Pinguin de Penachos Amarillos
Fuegian: Kalaouina
Maori: Tawaki, Pokotiwha

Length 63cm (25in). Distinguished from other crested penguins by smaller size, red eyes and drooping crest. Much confused with macaroni penguin.

Circumpolar in mainly temperate sub-Antarctic. Macquarie, Auckland, Campbell, Antipodes, Kerguelen, Tristan da Cunha, Falklands, Tierra del Fuego, etc.

Most aggressive of the penguins; will attack intruders with gusto, even jumping up to fasten to a sleeve and hold on furiously. Rookeries formed on rocky coastline. Two bluish-white eggs laid in a nest of pebbles or grass (according to terrain). Nests often in caves or crevices, or on open terraces. Breeding schedule varies according to location. Progresses in a series of bounds.

Predators: on land, skuas and gulls. At sea, leopard seals. Much exploited by man for eggs and oil in the past.

MACARONI PENGUIN *Eudyptes chrysolophus* (Brandt)
or Rockhopper (by confusion)
Spanish: Pinguin macaroni, Pinguin de Frente Amarilla

Length 66–76cm (26–30in). Larger than rockhopper, which it closely resembles and with which it is frequently confused. Plumes orange rather than yellow, extending backward rather than outward.

Sub-Antarctic islands in the Atlantic and Indian oceans. South Georgia, Kerguelen, Heard, South Shetland, South Orkney, Falkland, South Sandwich, Bouvet, Prince Edward and Crozet Islands.

Macaronis have a strong goatish smell. Bolder and tougher than their frequent neighbours, the gentoos. Rookeries established on coastal promontories or islets, sometimes consisting of many thousands of birds, sometimes only a few, when they join forces with rockhoppers particularly. May lay three eggs (chalky-white or very pale bluish-greenish), from which only one chick is likely to be reared. Nest of small stones, mud, tussock grass. Feeds on squid, shrimps.

Predators: skuas, sheathbills, leopard seals.

ROYAL PENGUIN *Eudyptes schlegeli* Finsch

Length 68–75cm (27–30in). The New Zealand equivalent of the macaroni penguin. Only crested penguin to have white cheeks and throat.

Large numbers breed on Macquarie Island. Also found on Campbell Island and to a smaller extent around the New Zealand coast.

Spends the period from May to September at sea. On Macquarie Island rookeries of up to half a million birds, covering as much as 6·7 hectares (16½ acres), form on coastal terraces. Two pale bluish eggs are laid in nest of small stones or even bones from penguin skeletons. Only one is incubated. Incubation period about five weeks. Male shares duties first ten days, then goes to sea, returning week before hatch;

he then guards chick for two to three weeks, when small crèches form. After moult all have gone to sea by end of April.

Southern skuas exploit royal penguins extensively, taking both eggs and young. Between 1894 and 1914 an important oil industry was based on this species, about 150,000 birds being taken every season without serious long-term effects on the population.

SNARES ISLAND PENGUIN *Eudyptes robustus*
or Snares Crested Penguin

Length 73cm (29in). Darker and larger than the very similar fiordland crested penguin. Also has heavier bill.

Breeds only at Snares Islands (south of New Zealand), but has been recorded on other New Zealand islands and mainlands.

After a winter at sea, large numbers arrive in August, to lay eggs in September. Dense rookeries are formed among the low scrub and tussock, along the line of creeks or waterways, up to 120m (400ft) above sea level. Two eggs laid in a substantial nest of sticks, lined with leaves and grass; the nest mounds stand out of a mess of filth and mud.

Rookeries are often close to breeding places of Hooker's sea-lions (*Phocarctos hookeri*). Sea-lions have been seen to chase penguins along the beach and then take them out to sea to eat, first tearing them to bits and discarding bones and skin, using a technique similar to that of the leopard seal.

YELLOW-EYED PENGUIN *Megadyptes antipodes*
(Hombron and Jacquinot)
or Yellow-crowned Penguin
Maori: Hoiho

Length 75cm (30in). Slate grey, with forehead and crown of pale gold with black stripes. Yellow eyes.

Sedentary, breeding only in the south-east area of New Zealand, including Auckland and Campbell Islands.

Rookeries on scrub and forest-covered slopes facing the sea. Up to a kilometre (half a mile) inland. Nest of sticks and coarse grass in holes or among rocks or scrub or forest. Two creamy-white eggs laid in September/October. Both incubated and two chicks reared normally. Incubation period forty to fifty days. Young are fully-fledged by about February. Moult takes place at the same site and the birds remain in the same area throughout the year, coming ashore every night. Feeds on squid and small fish.

Much persecuted by man.

LITTLE PENGUIN *Eudyptula minor* (Forster)
or Little Blue Penguin, Fairy Penguin
Sub-species: Cook Strait Blue Penguin, Northern Blue Penguin, Southern Blue Penguin, White-flippered Penguin
Maori: Korora

Length 40cm (16in). Smallest of all penguins. No crest. Slate blue. Chin, throat, neck and underparts white. Bill black, feet pale flesh, black soles. Eyes silver-grey.

Coasts and islands of Southern Australia from Perth to Brisbane (the only penguin at all common in Australia), Tasmania, New Zealand, Chatham Islands, etc.

Coastal species. Not gregarious. Nests (sticks, leaves, seaweed, grass) in crevices or burrows up to 1½km (1 mile) from the shore. Two white eggs. Incubation period about thirty-nine days.

Has suffered reduction in numbers through loss of habitat,

218

when scrub and forest has been cleared. Also killed by dogs, cats, stoats and ferrets, and run over by cars on coastal roads. Feeds on small fishes, swallowing them underwater.

JACKASS PENGUIN *Spheniscus demersus* (Linné)
or Black-footed Penguin, Spectacled Penguin, Cape Penguin

Length 63cm (25in). Slate coloured, but with the white of the breast extending in a semicircular pattern behind and over the head. Narrow black line in the shape of a horseshoe extends along the flanks and across the chest. Flesh-pink marking around and above the eye.

Sedentary. Confined to South African waters, bounded in the north by Mozambique and Angola. The majority of the species is found in the cooler waters of the Cape coast, breeding on the coast and islands, especially Dassen and Dyer Islands.

Highly gregarious at breeding time. Extended season, but November and March are the principal months. Nest of twigs, roots, weed, less often stones, in sand burrows (or rock cavities a foot or so deep) in the bare wind-swept terrain. Two greenish eggs, sometimes three or four. Incubation period twenty-eight days. Chick fed for as long as three months. Main food sources are pilchards ($33\frac{1}{3}$ per cent), maasbankers, anchovies, squid and crustaceans.

Predators: on land, dominican gulls, sacred ibis; at sea, octopus, shark. Much exploited by man, but conserved on account of its commercial significance as a guano and egg producer. (Numbers are controlled to placate the local fishing industry.)

PERUVIAN PENGUIN *Spheniscus humboldti* (Meyen)
or Humboldt Penguin
Spanish: Pajaro Niño
Indian: Petranca

Length 68cm (27in). Similar to the magellanic penguin, but without the broad band across the fore-neck. Narrower white superciliary stripe passing well above the eye. Bill heavier and longer.

Breeds on islands of the west coast of South America from Valparaiso (Chile) north along the Peruvian coast. Range is confined to the coastline served by the Humboldt current.

Breeding season extends throughout the year. Nests in caves and crevices, and in sand burrows. Two eggs. Feeds on the large shoals of small fish, such as anchovies, typical of the Humboldt current.

Exploited for the mineral-rich guano.

MAGELLANIC PENGUIN *Spheniscus magellanicus* (Forster)
or Magellan Penguin, Jackass Penguin
Spanish: Pajaro Niño, Pajaro Manco, Burro
Indian: Choncha

Lengths about 70cm (28in). Striking piebald plumage – even the bill is often flecked with white.

Breeds Falkland Islands and islands along the Patagonian coast from Lat. 41° S southward to Cape Horn, Staten Island and outlying islands. Ranges northward as far as southern Brazil.

Rookeries (warrens would be more appropriate in this case) are formed in a surprising variety of habitats – grassy slopes, woodland, peatbanks, sandhills and coastal bluffs. Nest of pebbles, twigs, leaves, feathers, forms a little mound anything up to 3m (10ft) inside the burrow, keeping the eggs above the water which sometimes accumulates. Two white eggs. Incubation period probably about twenty-eight days.

In the breeding season magellanic penguins feed on the cuttlefish which are found around the inshore kelp beds. At other seasons small fish.

GALAPAGOS PENGUIN *Spheniscus mendiculus* Sundevall

Length 50cm (20in). Smallest of the *Spheniscus* penguins, with the narrowest white head-stripe and almost entirely black flipper. Bill slender and relatively long. The characteristic white markings are mottled and less clear in this species. Weight 2·5kg (5½lb).

The only equatorial penguin. Confined to the Galapagos Islands, 970km (600 miles) west of Ecuador, where it is supported by the fertile, Antarctic-born Humboldt current. Found mainly in the southerly and westerly islands of the group. Rarest of all penguins, total population 1,000–2,000.

Breeding season May/July. Nest of a few stones arranged in a circle in caves and crevices, in the lava, sometimes as little as 90cm (3ft) above high-water mark. Frequently breeds alongside flightless cormorants or boobies. Feeds on small fish.

Sources

ANON. *The Antarctic Pilot*, Hydrographic Dept, Admiralty. London. 1948.

AUSTIN, O. L. 'Notes on banding birds in Antarctica and in the adélie penguin colonies of the Ross Sea Section', *Bird Banding* 28:1–26. 1957.

BAGSHAWE, T. W. 'Notes on the habits of the gentoo and ringed or Antarctic penguins', *Trans.* Zoological Society of London, 24:185–306. 1738.

BARTON, D. 'Swimming speed of a Little Penguin.' *Emu* 79:141–142. 1979.

BEAGLEHOLE, J. C. (ed). *The Journals of Capt. James Cook on his voyages of discovery.* Hakluyt Society and Cambridge University Press, 2 vols. 1955, 1961.

BEAGLEHOLE, J. C. (ed). *The Endeavour Journal of Joseph Banks,* 1768–1771. Angus & Robertson. 1962.

BEEBE, W. *Galapagos, World's End*, Putnam, 1924.

BOERSMA, P. D. 'An ecological and behavioural study of the Galapagos penguin.' *Living Bird* 15:43–93. 1976.

BOURNE, W. R. P. 'A review of oceanic studies of the biology of seabirds.' *Proc.* 13th International Ornithological Congress: 831–854. 1963.

BUDD, G. M. 'The biotopes of emperor penguin rookeries.' *Emu* 61:171–189. 1961.

BULLER, Sir W. L. *A History of the Birds of New Zealand.* London, 1888.

223

CAMPBELL, B. and LACK E. (Eds). *A Dictionary of Birds.* Poyser. 1985.

CARRICK, R. 'Problems of conservation in and around the Southern Ocean'. *Biologie Antarctique*, Hermann, Paris. 1962.

CHERRY-GARRARD, A. *The Worst Journey in the World*, Penguin Books. 1948.

COLEMAN-COOKE, J. *Discovery II in the Antarctic*, Odhams. 1963.

CONWAY, W. G. 'The penguin metropolis of Punto Tombo.' *Animal Kingdom*: 115–123. 1965.

CROXALL, J. P. 'Seabirds.' *Antarctic Ecology*, ed R. M. Laws. 2:533–619. London Academic Press. 1984.

CROXALL, J. P. and LISHMAN, G. S. 'The food and feeding ecology of penguins.'

CROXALL, J. P., RICKETTS, C. and PRINCE, P. A. 'The impact of seabirds in marine resources, especially Krill, at South Georgia.' *Seabird Energetics*, ed G. C. Whittow & H. Rahn. 285–318. New York Plenum Publishing Corporation. 1984.

CUAGHLEY, G. 'The adélie penguins of Ross and Beaufort Islands'. *Rec. Dom. Mus.* 3:263–282. 1960.

DARWIN, C. *The Voyage of the Beagle*. Dent. 1906.

DAVIES, S. J. J. F. *'Behaviour studies on Antarctic animals'*. *Biologie Antarctique*, Hermann, Paris. 1962.

DE BEER, G. 'The evolution of Ratites'. *Bull.* British Museum (Natural History) Zoological Service. 4:57–76. 1956.

DE BOUGAINVILLE, Louis. *A Voyage round the World.* London. 1772.

DE BRY, Theodore. *Grands Voyages*, Frankfurt. 1590–1634.

DE BRY, Theodore. *Petits Voyages*, Frankfurt. 1598–1628.

DOUGLAS, D. A. 'Extra-venal salt excretion in the adélie penguin chick'. *Biologie Antarctique*, Hermann, Paris. 1962.

D'URVILLE, Capt. DUMONT. *Voyage au Pole Sud et dans l'Oceanie*. Paris. 1841–5.

EDWARDS, G. *A Natural History of Uncommon Birds.* London. 1745.

EIBL-EIBESFELDT. I. *Galapagos.* Macgibbon & Kee. 1960.

EKLUND, C. R. 'Population studies of Antarctic seals and birds', *Biologie Antarctique*, Hermann, Paris. 1962.

EMLEN, J. T. and PENNEY, R. L. 'Distance navigation in the adélie penguin.' *Ibis* 106: 417–31. 1964.

FALLA, R. A. 'Distribution patterns of birds in the Antarctic and high-latitude sub-Antarctic', *Biologie Antarctique*, Hermann, Paris. 1962.

FALLA, R. A. 'Exploitation of seals, whales and penguins in New Zealand', *Proc.* New Zealand Ecological Society. 1962.

FALLA, R. A., SIBSON, R. B. and TURBOTT. *A Field Guide to the Birds of New Zealand*. Collins. 1966.

FANNING, Capt. Edmund. *Voyages Round the World*. London. 1834.

FORSTER, J. R. *Observations made during a Voyage round the World*. London. 1778.

FORSTER, J. R., *Commentationes Societatis Regiae Scientiarum Göttingensis*, Göttingen. 1781.

GILLHAM, M. E. *A Naturalist in New Zealand*. Museum Press. 1966.

GRAY, G. R. and SHARPE, R. B. *The Zoology of the Voyage of HMS Erebus and Terror*. London. 1846.

GWYNN, A. M. 'The egg-laying and incubation periods of rockhopper, macaroni and gentoo penguins'. *A.N.A.R.E. Reports*, Series B (1): 1–29. 1953.

HAGEN, Y. 'Birds of Tristan da Cunha'. No 20, *Results of the Norwegian Scientific Expedition to Tristan da Cunha 1937–8*. Det Norske Videnskaps – Akademi Oslo. 1952.

HAKLUYT, Richard (posthumus). *Hakluytus Posthumus, or Purchas his Pilgrimes*, London. 1624.

HAMPDEN, J. *Richard Hakluyt: Voyages and Documents*. Oxford University Press. 1958.

HARRINGTON, H. J. 'Adélie penguin rookeries in the Ross Sea region', *Notornis* 9: 33–9. 1960.

HAWKINS, Sir Richard. *The Observations of Sir Richard Hawkins, Knight, in his voyage to the South Sea, anno domini 1593*. London. 1622.

JOUVENTIN, P. *Visual and vocal signals in Penguins, their*

Evolution and Adaptive characters. Verlag Paul Pavey. 1982.

KEARTON, C. *The Island of Penguins.* Longmans. 1930.

KING, J. E. *Seals of the World.* British Museum (Natural History). 1964.

KINSKY, F. C. 'The yearly cycle of the northern blue penguin, *Eudyptula minor movaehollandiae,* in the Wellington Harbour area.' *Rec. Dom. Mus.* 3: 145–218. 1960.

KOOYMANS, G. L., DAVIS, R. W., CROXALL, J. P. and COSTA, D. P. 'Diving depths and energy requirements of King Penguins.' *Science* 217: 726–727. 1982.

LATHAM, J. *A General History of Birds.* London. 1824.

LEVICK, G. M. *Antarctic Penguins.* Heinemann. 1914.

LILLIE, H. R. *The Path through Penguin City.* Benn. 1955.

LUND, M. K. 'Penguins north of the polar circle', *Norsk Hualjangsstid* 44: (2) 95–100. 1955.

MOOREHEAD, A. *The Fatal Impact.* Hamish Hamilton. 1966.

MUNCH, P. A. 'Sociology of Tristan da Cunha'. No. 13, *Results of the Norwegian Scientific Expedition to Tristan da Cunha 1937–38.* Det Norske Videnskaps – Akademi Oslo. 1945.

MURPHY, R. C. *Oceanic Birds of South America.* Macmillan, New York. 1936.

MURPHY, R. C. 'Conservation of the Antarctic fauna'. *Biologie Antarctique,* Hermann, Paris. 1962.

MURPHY, R. C. 1958 'History of the Penguins', *Nat. Hist. N. Y.* 68: 152–60. 1958.

NELSON, B. *Seabirds, their biology and ecology.* Hamlyn. 1980.

NICHOLLS, B. 'An introduction to the study of the penguins in the Nobbies, Phillip Island, Western Point, Victoria.' *Emu* 17. 1918.

O'BRIEN, P. J. 'Some observations on the breeding habits and general characteristics of the white-flippered penguin (*Eudyptula albosignata* Finsch)', *Rec. Cant. Mus.* 4 (6): 311. 1940.

OLIVER, W. R. B., 'The crested penguins of New Zealand'. *Emu* 53: 185–188. 1953

OLIVER, W. R. B., *New Zealand Birds.* Reed, Wellington. 1955.

OSTENSIO, N. A. and SLADEN, W. L. J. 'Penguin tracks far inland in the Antarctic', *Auk* 77: 466–69. 1960.

PENNANT, T. *Philosophical Transactions*, London. 1768.

PENNEY, R. L. 'The adélie penguin's faithfulness to territory and mate.' *Biologie Antarctique*, Hermann, Paris. 1962.

PENNEY, R. L. 'Some practical aspects of penguin navigation – orientation studies', *Bioscience*, 15. 1965.

PENNEY, R. L. 'Voices of the adélie'. *Nat. Hist. N.Y.* 71: 16–25.

PETTINGILL, O. S. 'Crèche behaviour and individual recognitions in a colony of rockhopper penguins'. *Wilson Bulletin* 72: 213–21.

PETTINGILL, E. R. and O. S. *Penguin Summer*. Cassell, 1962.

PHILLIPS, A. 'A note on the ecology of the fairy penguin, *Eudyptula minor novaehollandiae* (Forster 1781), in Southern Tasmania', *Papers. Royal Society of Tasmania* 94: 63–72.

PRÉVOST, J. 'Ecologie du manchot empereur *Aptenodytes forsteri* Gray' *Publ. Exped. Polaires Françaises* 222. 1961.

PRÉVOST, J. 'How Emperor penguins survive the Antarctic climate', *New Scientist* 16: 444–7. 1962.

PRÉVOST, J. 'Influence des facteurs bio-climatiques sur le nomadisme des manchots empereurs à la colonie de Pointe Geologie', *Oiseau* 33: 89–102. 1962.

RAND, R. W. 'Some early references to the Cape Penguin', *Ostrich* 20: 2–5. 1949.

RAND, R. W. 'The biology of guano-producing seabirds. The distribution, abundance and feeding habits of the Cape penguin, *Spheniscus demersus*, off the south-western coast of Cape Province' *Invest. Rep. Div. Fish. S.Af.* No. 41: 1–28. 1960.

REILLY, P. N. and CULLEN, J. M. 'The little penguin *Eudyptula minor* in Victoria.' II: 'Breeding.' *Emu* 81: 1 81. III: 'Dispersal of chicks after banding.' *Emu* 82: 137–142. 1982.

RICHDALE, L. E. 'Random notes on the genus *Eudyptula* on the Otago Peninsula, New Zealand.' *Emu* 40: 180–217. 1940.

RICHDALE, L. E. 'A brief summary of the history of the

yellow-eyed penguin'. *Emu* 40. 1941.

RICHDALE, L. E. 'Erect-crested penguin (*Eudyptes sclateri* Buller)'. *Emu* 41: 25–53. 1941.

RICHDALE, L. E. 'Further notes on the erect-crested penguin'. *Emu* 49: 153–66. 1950.

RICHDALE, L. E. *Sexual behaviour in Penguins*. Lawrence, Kan. 1951.

RICHDALE, L. E. *A Population Study of Penguins*. Oxford University Press. 1957.

RIESENBERG, F. *Cape Horn*. Hale. 1941.

ROBERTS, B. 'Chronological List of Antarctic Expeditions'. *Polar Record* 9: 59. 1958.

RIVOLIER, J. *Emperor Penguins*. Elek. 1956.

ROSS, Capt. Sir James Clark. *A voyage of discovery and research in the southern and antarctic regions during the years* 1839–43. John Murray, London. 1847.

SAPIN-JALOUSTLE, J. 'Découverte et description de la rookerie des manchots empereurs de Pointe Geologie'. *Oiseau* 22: 143–84; 225–60. 1952.

SAPIN-JALOUSTRE, J. 'Ecologie du manchot adélie' *Publ. Exped. Polaires Françaises*, 208, 1960.

SCHMIDT-NIELSEN, K. and SLADEN, W. J. L. 'Nasal salt secretion in the humboldt penguin.' *Nature* 181: 1217–18. 1958.

SCOTT, P. and P. *Faraway Look Two*. Cassell, London. 1960.

SIMPSON, G. G. 'Fossil Penguins' *Bull. Amer. Mus. Nat. Hist.* 87: 9–99, 1946.

SIMPSON, G. G. *Penguins, Past & Present, Here and There*. Yale University Press. 1976.

SLADEN, W. J. L. 'The pygoscelid penguins' *Falkland Is. Dep. Surv. Sci. Rep.* 17: 1–97. 1958.

SLADEN, W. J. L. 'The distribution of the adélie and chinstrap penguins' in *Biologie Antarctique*, Hermann, Paris. 1962.

SLADEN, W. J. L. 'Ornithological research in Antarctica'. *Bioscience* 15 (4). 1965.

SONNERAT, P. *Voyage à la Nouvelle Guinée*, Paris. 1776.

SPARKS, J. H. 'Why no northern penguins?' *Animals* 8: (6) 150–5. 1966.

STONEHOUSE, B. (Ed). *The biology of Penguins.* London. Macmillan. 1975.

STONEHOUSE, B. 'The emperor penguin, *Aptenodytes forsteri* Gray. I – Breeding behaviour and development. *Falkland Is. Depend. Surv. Sci. Rep.* 6: 1–33. 1953.

STONEHOUSE, B. 'The King Penguin, *Aptenodytes patagonica* of South Georgia. I – Breeding behaviour and development.' *Falkland Is. Depend. Surv. Sci. Rep.* 23: 1–81. 1960.

STONEHOUSE, B. 'Observations on Adélie Penguins (*Pygoscelis adeliae*) at Cape Royds, Antarctica.' *Proc. XIII Internat. Orn. Congr. Ithaca N.Y.* 962: 1766–79. 1963.

STORER, R. W. 'Evolution in the diving birds' *Proc. XII Internat. Orn. Cong. Helsinki* 1958: 694–707. 1960.

TAYLOR, R. H. 'The Adélie Penguin, *Pygoscelis adeliae*, at Cape Royds' *Ibis* 104: 176–204. 1962.

THOMSON, A. L. (ed.) *A New Dictionary of Birds*, Nelson. 1964.

TULLOCK, A. 'Macquarie Island penguins', *Emu* 16. 1916.

WARHAM, J. 'Aspects of the biology of the Erected-crested Penguin *Eudyptes sclateri.*' Ardea 60: 145–184. 1972.

WARHAM, J. 'Breeding biology and behaviour of the Snares Crested Penguin.' *Journals of the Royal Society of New Zealand* 4: 63–108. 1974.

WARHAM, J. 'The nesting of the little penguin, *Eudyptula minor*', *Ibis* 100: 605–16, 1958.

WARHAM, J. 'The rockhopper penguin, *Eudyptes chrysocome*, at Maquarie Island', *Auk* 80: 229–56. 1963.

WEDDELL, Capt. James *A Voyage Towards the South Pole.* London. 1825.

WILLIAMS, A. J., COOPER, J., NEWTON, I.P., PHILLIPS, C. M. and WATKINS, B. P. *Penguins of the World: A Bibliography.* British Antarctic Survey. 1985.

WILLIAMS, A. J. and SIEGFRIED, W. R. 'Foraging ranges of Krill-eating penguins'. *Polar Record* 125: 159–162. 1980.

YOUNG, E. C. 'The breeding behaviour of the South Polar skua, *Catharacta maccormicki*', *Ibis* 105: 203–33. 1963.

ZEEK, P. M. 'Double trachea in penguins and sea lions', *Anatomical Record* 111: 327–43. 1951.

Appendix

Penguins in Captivity

Since the first edition of this book was published, there has been a significant shift in our attitude towards captive animals. Those who live in the developed countries have assumed a reverence for wild creatures, and this is enshrined in CITES, the Convention of International Trade in Endangered Species. The upshot of this Convention is that zoos can no longer rely upon a steady supply of freshly caught animals to replenish their stocks, and so they are increasingly addressing themselves to breeding programmes, thus becoming self-sustaining.

This is undoubtedly to the benefit of penguins. Although there is currently evidence of an illicit trade in these birds caught in nets by Asian mariners while fishing in the Southern Seas, the legal business is nowadays much reduced compared with that of two decades ago when, for instance, the late Len Hill, the proprietor of Birdland – a Cotswold menagerie – bought two islands. Part of the Falklands, Steeple and Jason sported handsome colonies of seabirds and little else. Mr Hill was a shrewd businessman and, with an eye on the clamorous hordes of rockhoppers, he conceived of ways of recouping his investment. He issued stamps bearing

The penguin enclosure designed by Ove Arup at the London Zoo; two inter-weaving stressed concrete ramps which are sprayed with water straddle the blue-tinted pool. When built in 1936 it was considered something of a revolution in the design of zoo displays although it is really too enclosed for penguins. The birds on the ramp are peruvians and jackass (right) (*Zoological Society of London*)

his own head, and visited his remote kingdom once a year to round up some of his flightless subjects and sold them to zoos. Valued at £50–100 per bird, Len's kingdom was worth a paper fortune, and he became dubbed the Penguin Millionaire'. Today his son carries on a modest trade, but in fertile eggs.

Relatively few people have the privilege of seeing penguins in the wild. The majority will only become acquainted with these birds in menageries. It might therefore be of interest to record some of the challenges faced by zoo directors in their quest to keep penguins alive and well in captivity. After all, a well-presented exhibit of these quaint creatures will keep the turnstiles clicking as well as almost any other kind of presentation.

Most of the problems for zoo directors arise out of the fact that many of the species of penguins offered them come from cool climates and therefore become easily hyperthermic and die of exhaustion. The severity of this problem will obviously depend upon the zoo's prevailing climate, and will be worse in those sub-tropically or tropically placed, where it may be necessary to display penguins in an expensive air-conditioned and perhaps refrigerated building. San Diego's Penguin Encounter is by far the most extravagant example. Costing $7 million, it is a vast chamber landscaped like a corner of Antarctica. Cooled to −2·2°C (28°F), 5,000kg (5 tons) of ice are sprayed daily onto a mixed bag of rockhoppers, emperors, kings and adélie penguins. A steady stream of visitors are carried along on a moving pavement, while video screens display pictures of penguins in the wild, and hidden speakers pour out a torrent of information. Behind the glass, the real penguins thrive in the hi-tech environment. Their 500,000 litre (100,000 gal) pool is filtered every 39 minutes, and the air is likewise recycled and sanitised. And it appears to have paid off because the emperor penguins have already reproduced – although during the last year or so the breeding seems to have unaccountably faltered.

Certain species suffer more from heat prostration than others. For example, the Ueno Zoological Garden in Tokyo

233

The penguin parade in the Scottish National Zoological Park, Edinburgh, with two gentoos and one chinstrap leading a gaggle of king penguins (*Paul Shillabeer*)

has a successful exhibit of nearly fifty penguins belonging to ten species; the king, macaroni, rockhopper, galapagos, magellan and peruvian penguins can be kept outside all the year round, the temperature varying from −6°C (21°F) to 36·5°C (98°F); the emperors and gentoos must be brought inside when the temperature is above 20°C (68°F), whereas the chinstraps and adélies have no tolerance of heat at all and are confined inside at a controlled temperature of between 15 and 18°C (59–64°F).

Whether inside or outside, penguins require a good supply of filtered cool water – not necessarily salt – and the pools should be deep and large enough for them to exercise in, and preferably arranged so that the onlookers can see them swimming beneath the water. Outside exhibits should include shaded areas and sprinklers to keep the surroundings cool, particularly in areas where the climate tends to be warm. Too many outside exhibits resemble pits, surrounded on all sides by concrete walls which act as heat traps and expose the birds to undue heat stress. In any case, to be boxed in must be psychologically wrong for them, because in their natural environment they spend most of their time on the sea, where the horizon is the limit.

Predictably, of course, the South African jackass and the more northern peruvian are more tolerant of high temperatures, and these are the two species most common in zoos. The more Antarctic species need special care, particularly the adélie and the emperor, though these are becoming more common in captivity. Blocks of ice are placed in the penguin exhibit at Hamburg Zoo, but in Duisberg, Milwaukee, Nagasaki, San Diego, Tokyo, and Amsterdam, and the Cheyenne Mountain Zoological Park, Colorado Springs, the penguins have their own refrigeration or air-conditioning plant or both. The precise temperatures maintained vary from one zoo to another. At Duisberg, which has a special polar exhibit, the pool temperature is kept between 9 and 12°C (48–54°F), whereas at Nagasaki, apparently, it is allowed up to 21°C (70°F), passing through the refrigerator four times a day.

If a collection of penguins is to thrive, the most vigorous standards of hygiene must be maintained, particularly as the birds are rather prone to diseases like *aspergillosis* for which there is no real cure. (They may even become infected in their natural habitat, and later develop resistance.) At the Tokyo Zoo, newly-arrived birds which may be suffering from *aspergillosis* are taken to a room where they are made to inhale 0·001 per cent of an anti-mould drug, Aureosryein, for periods of up to an hour for ten days. A fungus, *Aspergillus fumigatus* (sometimes *A. flavus*), is the causative agent and is cosmopolitan in its distribution; it grows in moist surroundings, for example on rotting seaweed, hay or even sacking, its spores being breathed in by the birds and lodging in the lungs and air sacs. The fungus grows and the air passages become coated with a cheese-like lining, which makes breathing difficult; the bird collapses and dies within a day or two.

Penguins should therefore be kept away from rotting vegetation, and of course air-conditioning measures like those adopted at Duisberg, where the air is filtered twelve times each hour, must be important life-savers; as always, prevention is better than cure. At Milwaukee, a positive air pressure is maintained in the exhibit, so that when the doors are opened dirt and uncleaned air from outside are prevented from flowing in; the keepers look more like surgeons with their white coats and face masks, and they must walk through disinfectant on the way in and out.

Sometimes the most suitable conditions for keeping penguins are discovered through trial and error. At Colorado Springs, a colony of king and peruvian penguins were moved to a new exhibit with a wetted non-skid tiled floor. Several birds developed pus-filled nodes on the feet, and in some cases these developed into lesions, affecting the joints of the leg. It became apparent that the continuously wet surface allowed the bacteria to enter the soles of the feet, and when the spray was kept off the floor the trouble disappeared. Even so foot care is essential, and in some zoos the feet are examined daily for signs of soreness through wear on wet concrete.

With hygiene and good sense, feeding is obviously a key to healthy birds. On the whole modern zoo practice favours individual feeding of penguins, particularly the larger species, to ensure that each one has its share. The smaller ones need about 0.5kg (1lb) of fresh fish daily, whereas the larger kings and emperors are fed anything between 1 and 2kg (2–4lb). This ration is increased by three or four times immediately preceding the moult. The fish must be of good quality, although there seems to be a considerable difference between zoos on the policy of feeding supplementary vitamins and minerals. For example, Chessington, Duisberg, Hamburg and Tokyo, all with fine penguin collections, give no additives. Yet the Amsterdam penguins receive Vitamins A, B^1, B^2, B^6, B^{12}, C, D^3, E. H and K, and also minerals, with their diet of herrings and whiting. More Vitamin A is given to the breeding pairs and chicks, a practice found to improve

Gentoo penguins nesting in the Scottish National Zoological Park, Edinburgh. There are some king penguins in the background (*Paul Shillabeer*)

their survival rate. The function of the nasal glands in excreting salt, acting as supplementary kidneys, has earlier been referred to; now the curator of birds at San Diego Zoo feels that the penguins in the collection remain healthier if their nasal glands are kept functioning. 1g pellets of sodium chloride are therefore inserted into individual fish and fed to all the penguins in the exhibit. In San Diego's experience a penguin should live from five to ten years in captivity – which would compare very creditably with the longevity records for some other zoological gardens, where survival for a year would be considered lucky.

It should be the policy of every zoo director to encourage his animals to breed, and it seems that penguins present no real difficulty if they are kept in good health in spacious compounds. In the United States of America, open-air exhibits have a greater breeding success than indoor ones. It goes without saying that small caves or burrows should be provided for the burrowing *spheniscus* species, which should have their entrances away from the public gaze. Of course the penguins adapt their breeding cycles to the northern hemisphere's spring and summer, so the king penguins usually commence laying between May and July. At Milwaukee Zoo, an adélie penguin laid in May 1966, only fifteen months after its arrival from Antarctica. At Nagasaki incubating king penguins are force-fed – a curious practice because it is normal for these birds to fast while incubating. Here a male took the first shift of thirty-three days, and the female relieved her mate for the last twenty days until the chick arrived. This particular pair laid again about twelve months later and apparently stopped feeding their chick when it was 170 days of age. However the keepers no doubt helped the parents by feeding their chick, and allowed the adults to commence breeding again rather earlier than would be natural for this species.

Acknowledgments

Many people have helped with this book, and we should particularly like to record our debt to the librarians and library staff of the Bodleian Library, the British Museum (Natural History), the Marine Biological Association of the United Kingdom, the Scott Polar Research Institute, the Zoological Society of London, and Devon County Library (Kingsbridge branch). Robert Gillmor, whose art work embellishes the pages, was indefatigable in his quest for accuracy and in making helpful suggestions; we also owe much to Andrew Pearson, who was all too easily persuaded to neglect his career and unravel some of the tangled threads of penguin history.

JOHN SPARKS
TONY SOPER

Index

Page numbers in *italic* indicate illustrations

241